Kathleen Burns Kingsbury's book *How to Give Financial Advice to Couples* gives real, practical advice on how to interact with couples. The importance of engaging both relationships and helping them understand their individual and shared money dynamics allows advisors to truly provide comprehensive planning and advice. Not only does Kathleen teach the differences between what happens in each member of a couple's brain, she provides advisors with action steps to take to ensure they are not part of the 70% who get fired when relationships end.

Kate Healy, Managing Director,
Institutional Marketing, TD Ameritrade

Financial advisors may not be marriage therapists, but financial planning done poorly can drive clients to need one! In her book, Kathleen Burns Kingsbury provides guidance on the essential skills advisors need to develop to navigate this delicate balance, and in the process create deeper, stronger relationships with their client couples—relationships that can survive difficult family transitions as couples become widows and divorcees as well.

Michael E. Kitces, CFP, Partner, Pinnacle Advisory
Group and Publisher of the Nerd's Eye View Blog

What a terrific book! Empowering women financially can only happen if you also empower the couple to work together as partners. *How to Give Financial Advice to Couples* is the perfect resource for financial advisors dedicated to better serving women and those they love.

Barbara Stanny, Author, *Prince Charming Isn't Coming,*
Overcoming Underearning, and *Secrets of Six-Figure Women*

Working effectively with couples is one of the biggest challenges faced by financial planners. In *How to Give Financial Advice to Couples,* Kathleen Burns Kingsbury has created a desperately needed resource to equip financial planners with the theories and techniques they need to help couples navigate life's biggest stressor—their relationship with money.

Brad Klontz, Psy.D., CFP, Financial Psychologist,
Associate Professor in Personal Financial
Planning, Kansas State University

This book is a strong reminder that clients need our respect and our listening skills as much as they need our financial expertise. It is a valuable resource for financial professionals, especially those wanting to offer client-focused financial planning.

Richard S. Kahler, MS, CFP, CCIM
Kahler Financial Group, Author, *Conscious Finance,* and
Co-author, *The Financial Wisdom of Ebenezer Scrooge*

This is a timely and important book on a subject that challenges the best financial counselors and advisors.

Kathleen Gurney, Ph.D., CEO Financial Psychology
Corporation and Author, *Your Money Personality:*
What It Is and How You Can Profit from It

This book is a must-read for any financial advisor. Savvy financial advisors will appreciate the easy-to-use and practical tools provided and be empowered to avoid the traps that derail too many client–financial advisor relationships.

John "John A" Warnick, Attorney at Law,
Founder of the Purposeful Planning Institute

How to Give Financial Advice to Couples is a must-read for financial services professionals looking to be on the cutting edge of their profession. Kathleen's easy-to-read style and real-life examples make this an interesting read and a must-have for advisors looking to grow and expand their business.

Meridith Elliott Powell, Founder, Motion
First and Author, *Winning in the
Trust & Value Economy*

How to Give Financial Advice to Couples is a Godsend. It has given our practice a better way to communicate and is prominently placed on our bookshelf as a valuable reference for years to come.

William Harris, CFP, WH Cornerstone
and Board Member, Massachusetts
Financial Planning Association

Money talks can be the most challenging aspect of interpersonal relationships, and Kathleen's latest book offers insights on advising couples in a way that honors their differences and encourages collaborative action. If you are already advising couples or plan to, this book is full of stories and skills to help you recognize your ability to meet couples where they are, fully explore their individual and shared concerns, and offer actionable advice.

Sandra Davis, MS, Financial Coach, Educator

With so many of our clients being couples, understanding those dynamics and the implications for advice givers is fundamental to doing it well. Kathleen Burns Kingsbury has created an invaluable resource for every advisor who works with couples.

Stephen Wershing, CFP, President,
The Client Driven Practice and Author,
Stop Asking for Referrals!

In this book, *Financial Advice for Couples*, Kathleen Burns Kingsbury has provided an invaluable resource for advisors working with high-net worth couples. Since couples conflict is the number-one source of marital discontent these days, every advisor would do well to read and incorporate the tools and dynamics explained so clearly in this excellent book.

Olivia Mellan, investment advisor columnist,
psychotherapist, and money coach,
and author of *Money Harmony*

HOW *to* GIVE FINANCIAL ADVICE *to* COUPLES

Essential Skills for Balancing
High-Net-Worth
Clients' Needs

Kathleen Burns Kingsbury

New York Chicago San Francisco Athens London Madrid Mexico City
Milan New Delhi Singapore Sydney Toronto

1 2 3 4 5 6 7 8 9 0   DOC/DOC   1 9 8 7 6 5 4 3

ISBN 978-0-07-181911-4
MHID 0-07-181911-8

e-ISBN 978-0-07-181912-1
e-MHID 0-07-181912-6

This publication is designed to provide accurate and authoritative information in regard to the subject matter covered. It is sold with the understanding that neither the author nor the publisher is engaged in rendering legal, accounting, securities trading, or other professional services. If legal advice or other expert assistance is required, the services of a competent professional person should be sought.
—*From a Declaration of Principles Jointly Adopted by a Committee of the American Bar Association and a Committee of Publishers and Associations*

McGraw-Hill Education books are available at special quantity discounts to use as premiums and sales promotions or for use in corporate training programs. To contact a representative, please visit the Contact Us pages at www.mhprofessional.com.

For My Husband

Contents

Acknowledgments

WRITING A BOOK IS A WILD RIDE BEST TRAVELED WITH GOOD friends, family, and colleagues. I was fortunate to have the support of so many talented and caring people for this second journey writing for McGraw-Hill. Thank you to all, especially:

To Jennifer Ashkenazy, my acquisition editor, and all the staff at McGraw-Hill, for your continued belief in my abilities to meet a deadline, to write a good business book, and to market the heck out of it when it is done!

To Ken Lizotte for first introducing me to the great folks at McGraw-Hill and for laughing at the crazy idea of publishing this next book so soon after the first, but still helping me pen a deal.

To Lauren Fleming for helping me spread the word about my first book, *How to Give Financial Advice to Women*, and for being excited to work together on this new one.

To Tom Crowell, my research assistant, for providing me with structure, and reminding me that attention to detail is a necessary evil. You jumped into this project head first and made this book better as a result.

To Suzanne Slater for your time and insights into same-sex couplehood. Your knowledge runs deep, and I can't wait to support you when you write your next book.

To the many powerful women in my life, especially Wendy Hanson, Meridith Powell, and Lauran Star; every day I am thankful for having all of you in my life to make me laugh when I want to pull out my hair and for cheering me on every step of the way.

To Denise Federer, Eleanor Blayney, and Shell Tain for providing your insights and expertise to this project; chatting and connecting with each of you feeds my soul.

To Kathy Goughenour, my assistant extraordinaire, for running the KBK Wealth Connection ship when I was too busy writing to be at the helm.

To Kelly Pelissier, my graphic designer, for using my words to create your pretty pictures, and for engaging in tangential conversations as if they related to the work at hand.

To the men and women who volunteered to be interviewed for this book. The topic of money is not always easy to talk about, and I am forever grateful for your candor about how money works in your relationships.

To Ellie and Bill, aka mom and dad, for showing me how to be in love, balance a checkbook, and manage money as a team.

To Team Kingsbury; together we are better than one, and I am forever grateful that your sailboat docked next to mine that fateful day in Block Island. It is no coincidence that I signed this book deal on our fifteenth wedding anniversary; just like us, it was meant to be.

Introduction

MOST FINANCIAL ADVISORS WORK WITH COUPLES IN THEIR PRACTICE every day. However, very few are formally trained in couple dynamics and how to effectively balance each individual's needs with those of the couple. As someone trained in psychology and family dynamics, I am surprised by how little the topic of couples and money is actually discussed in the industry. I surmise that prior to the global financial crisis in 2008, advisors did not need to focus on advising couples effectively because revenues were high and clients were complacent. Or maybe it is part of the industry's failure to view and include female clients in the investment process. If only the male client counts, why even try to understand the relationship between the two?

Whatever the reason, the proverbial elephant in the room is that the majority of clients seeking financial advice are couples. These couples have complex attitudes and values concerning money that you need to understand, appreciate, and work with in designing a financial plan or investment strategy. In addition, the nature of couplehood in our society is changing. No longer are all marriages between a man and a woman. Many couples are having children before they walk down the aisle, and many more are opting to live together instead of legally tie the knot. Gender roles are not set in stone, with the number of stay-at-home dads increasing and breadwinner wives becoming more commonplace. With these society shifts comes a greater need for advisors to be skilled in interviewing couples about their thoughts and beliefs about money, facilitating financial conversations, and mediating differences between partners. At the same time, clients are demanding more from their financial advisors and want long-term client–advisor relationships focused on their ever-changing goals and objectives.

As I traveled the country promoting my previous book, *How to Give Financial Advice to Women: Attracting and Retaining High-Net-Worth Female Clients*, audiences and readers repeatedly shared their struggles with me about advising couples. The questions I heard over and over included, "How do I encourage my female client to speak up in meetings when her husband dominates the conversation?," "How do I get both members of the couple to actually show up for meetings?," and "What do I do if one member of the couple is financially literate and the other one is not?" This book is written to answer these questions and many more.

I felt that writing this book about couples now was an important next step in my work empowering women and the advisors who serve them. Not only is there a need in the marketplace for more information, but I have a desire to share what I know about couple dynamics to make sure the women you work with receive the best quality financial services possible. Many women come into your office with their partners, and you need to be prepared to meet and exceed not only her needs, but his too. Doing so is not only good for her and her partner, but also good for your business. Currently, only 30 percent of women retain their financial advisor after the death of their spouse.[1] This is a startling statistic that highlights how risky it is to not be proficient in communicating and working with both members of a couple.

How to Give Financial Advice to Couples: Essential Skills for Balancing High-Net-Worth Clients' Needs is written for financial services professionals looking to better understand and serve their couple clients. The book offers insights into the complex world of couplehood and how advisors can help clients navigate their financial lives together. While this is at times challenging, the reward to the advisor can be great. Not only will you be more successful in developing financial plans and investment strategies that work, but you will be more likely to retain the individual members of the couple during times of family transition, such as death or divorce.

How to Give Financial Advice to Couples is broken into two sections. The first section, "The Psychology of Couples," discusses the challenges and rewards in working with couples, the common myths about couples and money, how couples operate as a system, and the typical life stages of partnership. Section II, "Essential Skills for Couple-Friendly Advisors," offers strategies for building and maintaining trust with both members of the couple, techniques for facilitating financial conversations and mediating differences, and tips for empowering parents to rear financially intelligent children. Finally, a chapter on special issues that can arise when advising couples is included.

It is worth mentioning that *How to Give Financial Advice to Couples* includes generalizations about male and female behaviors. Some facts are presented in a simplistic way to make a point or teach a concept. Please keep in mind that as with any conversation about gender, some of the information may apply to your clients and some may not. Make sure you always view your male and female clients as individuals first and members of a gender second.

I hope you enjoy and benefit from reading *How to Give Financial Advice to Couples*. Like you, I am an entrepreneur who is always learning more about how to best serve my clients; therefore, I welcome your feedback. Please e-mail me at kbk@kbkwealthconnection.com with your thoughts on the book and how your clients react to the tools and tips offered. Also feel free to check out my company's website at http://www.kbkwealthconnection.com. It is constantly being updated with articles, blogs, and other useful tools for advisors as well as clients.

Until then, happy reading!
Kathleen

The Psychology of Couples

1

The Financial Advisor's Dilemma

Sometimes questions are more important than answers.

—Nancy Willard, American poet and writer

ADVISING COUPLES IS AN ART, NOT A SCIENCE. IT REQUIRES AN understanding of couple and family dynamics and gender differences. As an advisor, you are required to be part mediator, part facilitator, and part objective observer. You can't take sides, even if you want to, and you need to keep your own judgments and opinions as to how a couple should operate out of the picture. Advising couples is challenging and offers its fair share of advisor dilemmas.

Imagine you are sitting in your office with a new couple prospect: a husband and wife who have been married for 10 years and have two children, ages five and seven. They came in to find out how you can help them save enough money to send their children to college and still live the lifestyle they currently enjoy. The husband, the CEO of his own company, does most of the talking, and his wife listens attentively. You assume that she is in agreement with what her husband wants for the family, but you don't ask her directly. You sense that he calls the shots, and you don't want to rock the boat so early in the process. The meeting ends, and you feel pretty confident that this couple will retain you to help them with their financial plan and college saving strategy. A week later, you follow up with a quick e-mail and find out that they decided to work with another advisor. When you ask why, the husband tells you that his wife didn't feel included in the conversation. He states, "She just didn't feel like she could trust you, but I thought your recommendations were spot on."

This is one of many scenarios where you, as the advisor, face a dilemma when meeting with couples. How do you balance her needs with his needs and then also factor in what makes sense for the couple? Do you let the verbally dominant spouse run the meeting? Do you encourage the quiet one to speak up? How do you quickly assess how the couple operates around money and then work with that dynamic? What if one client is more financially literate than the other? Do you cater to the one who is more financially savvy or bring the bar down to accommodate the less literate partner? The questions are endless.

Finding the answers is no easy task. As a financial advisor, you are forced to quickly assess the best tack to take with couples, often without having adequate training in understanding and working with couple dynamics. Chances are you were coached to pay more attention to the male wealth creator than to his wife. The historical belief is that the husband makes the financial decisions for the family and the wife really is not that interested in money management and investments. Although this may be the case with some couples, especially those who are from older generations, it is a risky assumption to make.

Over the past decade, there has been a shift in gender roles in families, making it no longer a given that the husband is the one who is making and managing the money. In 1970, women in the United States contributed 2 to 6 percent to the family income. Now the average American wife contributes 42.2 percent.[1] Furthermore, almost 40 percent of U.S. wives outearn their husbands.[2] Women make 80 percent of household buying decisions, including whom to hire for financial services, even if they do not overtly demonstrate this power in the meeting.[3] Don't be fooled by appearances. A woman may be polite and gracious in a meeting and then, on the car ride home, veto her husband's decision to hire you. Although he may call you to let you know she is the one who doesn't want to work with you, he may be relieved, as he really wants an advisor who will take care of his wife if he dies first. If you don't connect with her as well as him, he may question whether you are the right advisor for the job.

How do you solve this dilemma? The answer lies in learning to develop a relationship with both partners simultaneously and remaining an objective observer of the couple's dynamics with regard to communication, task completion, and money management. Few advisors are trained in these skills or encouraged to develop this type of expertise. The result is that 70 percent of widows fire the couple's advisor within one year of the death of their spouse.[4] What this alarming statistic shows is that the financial services industry is failing to support not only the women they serve, but also the men in the lives of those women. Something is amiss in the advisor–couple relationship if such a high percentage of female clients walk out the door so soon after their husbands or partners are no longer with them.

In my book *How to Give Financial Advice to Women: Attracting and Retaining High-Net-Worth Female Clients*, I explain that women feel overlooked and discounted by the financial services industry. They don't feel they are being seen and valued as real partners in the management of the family finances. This leads to resentment and a belief that financial advisors cater only to men. Although historically, this may have been the case because the men held the wealth, this is no longer true. In recent years, the industry has started to stand up and take notice of the economic power of women, but it still has a long way to go. Many financial firms have launched initiatives to reach out to the "women's market." This strategy, while well-intended, offends female clients, as these women want to be seen as unique individuals with diverse needs, not members of one big homogeneous group. The idea of a "men's market" sounds absurd. So too is the idea of a "women's market." Other firms mistakenly have decided that female clients' dissatisfaction is an issue to be delegated to women advisors only. This approach ignores the data showing that most women want trustworthy, credible financial advisors and gender is a factor for only a small percentage of these clients. Finally, most financial advising firms have given very little thought to the special needs of women in couples. Given the fact that a large majority of female clients hire financial advisors jointly with their partners, it is vital to develop, implement, and train advisors in best practices for effectively advising women in couples too.

Don't be mistaken. This is not just a women's issue. Men are being left out of the conversation as well. The women I interviewed for this book often complained that their husbands wouldn't go to the financial advisor with them. I also heard from financial advisors who were frustrated, but complacent, with only meeting with the wife. Yes, there is a big problem in this industry when it comes to effectively advising women, but it is only part of the picture when it comes to the failure of the industry to advise couples effectively. This is actually an equal opportunity problem that is not gender specific.

In Her Own Words

We are fifty-fifty with everything else—cooking, cleaning, childcare—but not with money. He prefers I take care of it, and I want him to share the responsibility with me.

—*Kelly, 38-year-old married business owner and mother of two*

Couples often give good reasons for not showing up together. She needs to work late. He is busy coaching the kid's soccer team. Yes, couples are busy. They often use the "divide and conquer" method of getting things done on the home front. This means that, at some point in time in their partnership, they made an agreement, either overtly or implicitly, to split the tasks. Often this division of labor is based on the skills of each member. For example, my husband fixes all the computer problems in the house, and I handle all the healthcare issues. Why? Because he is very tech savvy and I have a background in healthcare. Did we sit down and make a concrete plan as to who would conquer various tasks in our lives? No. But like most couples, we naturally fall into patterns based on our strengths.

The same phenomenon happens in couples when it comes to managing money. The spouse who is the financially savvy one typically takes the lead. This person, man or woman, tends to talk more in financial meetings and is your primary contact. You may be thinking, what is the problem if it works? The problem is that financial decisions ideally are tied to life goals and aspirations, and one person cannot do the talking for two. Also, when it comes to money, partners are often not honest with each other. An article in *Kiplinger's* magazine reported that 80 percent of Americans admit that they keep financial secrets from their spouses and significant others.[5] When you are communicating to one spouse, how can you be sure the information is being accurately portrayed to the other when so many clients struggle to be truthful about finances? And even if they are honest with each other, your intent can be easily lost in translation. A couple-friendly advisor requires both members of the couple to be present for these discussions. One without the other is not sufficient.

The other reason couples may not want to meet with you as a team is exactly why they should. Talking about money and finances can be emotional. Many spouses avoid these conversations outside of your office, so why not in your office as well? This is where you can provide value. The number one stressor in many couples' lives is making, spending, and managing money together. Fifty percent of all first marriages end in divorce, many of them because of financial stress.[6] Therefore, couples need to be strongly encouraged to work together financially, to show up at your office as a unit, and to learn to make financial decisions jointly. Although you are not a marriage counselor, you are often the one and only professional who talks to the couple about the sensitive but important topic of money.

IN HIS OWN WORDS

I bring up money when I feel I have no choice but to discuss it with my wife.
—MATT, 40-YEAR-OLD MARRIED SOCIAL WORKER AND FATHER OF TWO

Working with couples requires a different skill set from giving financial advice to an individual male or female client. Individual client communication is linear. You ask a question, the client answers. The client speaks, you listen. Easy! However, couples' communication is complicated. Two individuals are talking and sharing a story, each with unique perspectives, money histories, and ideas about what financially makes sense for them individually and together. Sometimes they agree. More often than not, their opinions diverge. Take retirement, for example:

◆ Fifty-three percent of couples approaching retirement don't agree on the age at which they will retire.
◆ Forty-seven percent of couples approaching retirement don't agree on whether they will continue to work in retirement.
◆ One in five couples don't agree on or don't know where they will live during this phase of their life.[7]

Although this is only one aspect of financial planning, it does highlight how working with couples requires an advisor to carefully gather data about how each member of the couple feels about his or her financial future. You must work to help the couple find a solution that both members can live with.

In Her Own Words

I would love to have my financial advisor give me the same level of attention that he gives to my husband. I am the primary breadwinner, but when the advisor calls, he only talks with my husband.

—KATHY, 56-YEAR-OLD MARRIED BUSINESSWOMAN

When done well, this type of guidance is invaluable for couples. It increases intimacy in the couple and the likelihood that your recommendations will be successful. It is also a great way for you as an advisor to differentiate your practice in a crowded marketplace. It is unfortunate that many advisors don't work with couples effectively, but it is also a business opportunity for those who do.

Becoming a Couple-Friendly Advisor

Let's face it. It is easier to advise one person than two. What the person in front of you wants is what you provide. You conduct an interview, review the client's financial information, and develop a financial plan and investment strategy to achieve his or her goals. Done!

With a couple, the practice of advising is more complex. You have two people in the meeting, two perspectives about money, multiple life visions, and two risk tolerance levels. Sometimes they overlap quite a bit, and sometimes they don't. Each question has at least two answers, and often the financial solutions lie somewhere in between the answers. Some couples will be forthright and honest when they communicate with you in a meeting. Others will be reluctant to share their opinions for fear of upsetting their partners. It is no wonder that many in the financial services industry prefer to work with just the husband or the wife. It certainly is less challenging.

IN HIS OWN WORDS

My wife has a very risk-averse personality, but I embrace calculated risk.

—ROBERT, 62-YEAR-OLD MARRIED INHERITOR AND BUSINESSMAN

While working primarily with one member of the couple is more clear-cut, it means that you are getting only half of the story and building a relationship with only one person. You run the risk of not really understanding the financial needs of the couple and making a recommendation that is less effective or, worse yet, inappropriate. You also are in danger of losing the couple client when one of them leaves the picture, either through death or through divorce. Finally, routinely meeting with only one person in a couple raises questions as to whether and how you can fulfill your fiduciary responsibility to the one who is not in the room.

The answer to this quandary is to become a couple-friendly advisor. A couple-friendly advisor is defined as a financial services professional who understands couple dynamics and is able to balance the financial needs of each individual member of the partnership with those of the couple as a whole. Being a couple-friendly advisor requires learning about the psychology of couples and how to work with the dynamics that are inevitably present when advising intimate partners. It also means mastering the communication skills needed to effectively facilitate couple financial conversations so that you can design strategies that serve all parties involved. Finally, it means being comfortable working with traditional couples as well as modern families that may have lifestyles that are vastly different from your own.

The good news is that advisors who skillfully and routinely advise couples find this work very rewarding. It can be deeply satisfying to witness a couple learning to talk more openly about money or figuring out how to resolve their differences to achieve a common goal. In a society that still finds talking about money taboo, being able to assist clients in understanding their money histories and how these impact their current financial habits is gratifying. Often you discover that this is the first time the couple has really discussed what money means to them and shared their thoughts and beliefs with each other. This ultimately increases the intimacy in the couple and the bond of trust and loyalty they feel toward you. At times it requires more effort, but the return on investment is very high. It would be wonderful if the knowledge and skills needed to become a couple-friendly advisor were widely taught in the field. But they are not. Therefore, I have written this book to teach you the skills needed to be successful at advising couples and to hopefully start a movement toward training advisors how to be proficient in this area. Some of this information may confirm what you know to be true intuitively. Other parts may be new to you. By reading the forthcoming chapters, you will learn how to include your female clients in the conversation, how to facilitate meaningful dialogues about money and wealth, and how to assist your couple clients with a variety of financial and life challenges over their lifespans. In the end, you will no longer find meeting with couples more work than meeting with individual clients. Instead you will think, "I can't imagine doing it any other way."

Summary

Practicing in a couple-friendly way is not only good for your clients, but good for your business. By attending to both partners' needs in the meeting and including both in the discussion, you decrease the risk of alienating one of the partners, especially the female client. At the same time, you increase the likelihood that her partner will trust you to help her should this person pass first. When a couple hires you and trusts you, you acquire more assets—his, hers, and theirs. Not only is this approach client-centric, but it is also likely to increase the longevity of your business.

Your Next Step: Your Couple-Friendly Quotient

How couple-friendly is your current advising practice? Find out by circling "True" or "False" in the following list. To get an accurate assessment, mark your responses according to your current practice, not based on what you think is the right answer. At the end, find out how to score this assessment to reveal your couple-friendly quotient (CFQ).

1. The person in the financial meeting who is more financially literate is the one whom I interact with the most. | True | False

2. In meetings, I help clients talk more openly about money even when they disagree. | True | False

3. Couples tend to balance each other out in terms of financial habits and behaviors. | True | False

4. If I see an older couple, I assume the man makes all the investment decisions. | True | False

5. Women who don't attend meetings are not interested in their finances. | True | False

6. When a female client nods, she is agreeing with what I am recommending. | True | False

7. Couples who truly love each other commingle their accounts. | True | False

8. If a client is clearly struggling with an addiction, I tend to look the other way, as this is not part of my job as a financial advisor. | True | False

9. When I meet with a couple, I try to position the female client across the table from me and the male client beside me or at a slight angle from where I am seated. | True | False

10. I use definitive statements when I share information in meetings and compare the clients' performance results to benchmarks such as Standard & Poor's. | True | False

11. I make an effort to ask the same question of both members of the couple in meetings. | True | False

12. In meetings, one member of the couple is dominant in the discussion and often is the only one who attends meetings regularly. | True | False

13. My office addresses all correspondence to both members of the couple. | True | False

14. If a client looks bored or distracted in a meeting, I assume that he or she is just not interested in the family finances. | True | False

15. My marketing material speaks to the common financial problems of the couples I serve. | True | False

16. My website has resources on how to raise financially literate children, how to have healthy money conversations, and how to better understand your partner's money personality. | True | False

17. Nontraditional couples are defined as same-sex couples. | True | False

18. If a woman is the breadwinner of the family, then she also makes the majority of the financial decisions.　　True　False

19. I have a written policy outlining my couple philosophy, and I share this with my clients at the first meeting as a way of setting clear expectations.　　True　False

20. I have life experience as a member of a couple that informs my work.　　True　False

Your Score

Give yourself 2 points for each of the following answers and then add up the total points to find out your CFQ.

1. False	6. False	11. True	16. True
2. True	7. False	12. False	17. False
3. True	8. False	13. True	18. False
4. False	9. True	14. False	19. True
5. False	10. False	15. True	20. True

CFQ Range

36–40 Points	Congratulations! You are a couple-friendly advisor.
22–34 Points	Nice job. You are well on your way to being a couple-friendly advisor, but you can still pick up a few tips.
0–20 Points	You have some work to do, but you can raise your CFQ simply by reading this book and completing each of the "Your Next Step" coaching exercises at the end of each chapter.

2

Myths About Couples and Money

Perhaps it is our imperfections that make us so perfect for one another!

—Jane Austen, English novelist

WHAT REALLY HAPPENED TO CINDERELLA AFTER SHE MARRIED Prince Charming? Did she live happily ever after? Or did she, like most wives, disagree from time to time with her husband about how to spend the kingdom's money? Did Prince Charming handle the finances alone, or did he prefer to share wealth management decisions with his new bride? Did they discuss money during their courtship, or were they too caught up in falling in love to think about such mundane tasks? My guess is how they were going to manage money as a couple didn't enter their minds until after they walked down the aisle and said "I do." Why should Cinderella and Prince Charming be any different from the majority of couples?

Fairy tales such as Cinderella, Snow White, and Sleeping Beauty are great stories and fun to share with our children. But these tales perpetuate societal myths about couples and money. These myths teach young boys and girls that romantic love involves women being financially rescued by men and that true love ends up with you and your partner living happily ever after. Unfortunately, there have been many women (and some men) who have relied on these myths as an investment strategy for the future and ended up broke, single, and very unhappy. Furthermore, the pressure involved in saving another person financially is exhausting and often leads to resentment in the relationship. The truth is, romantic love blossoms into mature love when two people make a commitment to work together financially. The healthiest couples identify their money beliefs, work to understand their shared values, and spend a lifetime living happily ever after negotiating and resolving financial differences.

As a financial advisor, you see how this myth and others play out in your office daily. Chances are you have worked with couples who are unrealistic about what it takes to reach their financial goals and believe their love will get them through, not good financial planning and discipline. Or you have advised a spouse who insists that he can rescue his wife from her spending habits. Or you have felt for the divorced woman who really thought she had met her Prince Charming, only to find out he truly was a toad. Although on the surface these myths appear harmless, they contribute to many couples, some of whom are your clients, failing to act as responsible adults around money and doing the hard work of managing finances together.

Folklore about couples and money abounds in our culture. Just turn on the television set, go to the movies, or read a good book, and you will witness how these half-truths about love and wealth are perpetuated in subtle and not-so-subtle ways. The following myths about couples and money need to be busted wide open if your client couples are going to take care of themselves financially.

Myth 1. Love conquers all. The Latin phrase "omnia vincit amor" dates back to the Roman poet Virgil and his work *Eclogue X*, written around 44 BC. Caravaggio used the saying to name his painting in 1601, and the rock band Deep Purple used the same phrase to name their song in 1990. Although it sounds good, is it true? Does love really conquer all?

Love does not conquer all when it comes to managing money together. I have worked with many couples who truly love each other but struggle to overcome their different viewpoints on how to spend, save, and invest money. When it comes to couples and money, it is important to know that love can have very little to do with it. It is more about shared values, respect for different money beliefs and money histories, and an appreciation that these diverse perspectives help the couple make the best possible financial decisions for their family. Hard work and the help of a couple-friendly financial advisor are what couples really need to conquer the challenges of managing money together. While loving your partner helps, it is not a guarantee.

Myth 2. Love means never having to say you're sorry. This is the famous phrase from the heartbreaking 1970 movie *Love Story*, starring actors Ryan O'Neal and Ali MacGraw. The movie is based on a novel by the same name and is about two people from different economic backgrounds who fall in love, get married, and struggle to make ends meet. The tale turns tragic when the couple learns the wife is dying of cancer. When the husband apologizes for getting angry, the sick wife utters, "Love means never having to say you're sorry." This classic line has been repackaged into song lyrics and even mocked in a later movie by O'Neal called *What's Up, Doc.* In it, his colead, Barbra Streisand, delivers the line, and O'Neal's character responds with, "That is the stupidest thing I have ever heard."

While loving someone does make it easier to forgive, it is important that couples learn how to apologize to each other. When it comes to finances, it is human to mess up. Just look at all the behavioral finance research supporting the idea that smart, rational people make stupid financial decisions when emotions are involved. When this happens, or when someone in a relationship gets hurt because of a money decision, love means you care enough to say you are sorry.

If couples learned how to apologize and forgive more readily when it came to financial matters, the divorce rate just might go down!

Myth 3. Happily married couples are open and honest about money. When you exchange marital vows, you are proclaiming to the world your love for your partner. For many, this implies that you trust that person with your heart. But should you trust your wife or husband with your wallet? According to a 2010 survey conducted by CESI Debt Solutions, 80 percent of all married people surveyed hide some purchases from their partners.[1] While both genders participate in this practice, men engage in keeping financial secrets more often than women. Figure 2.1 summarizes the findings by type of expenditure and gender.

Figure 2.1

What Purchases Spouses Hide

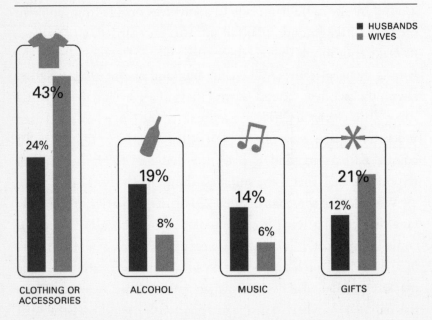

Source: CESI Debt Solutions.

What about larger decisions? Do marital couples hide financially large purchases from each other? According to one tax accountant I interviewed, the answer is a resounding "yes". She stated, "My favorite story involves a friend who loved the old VW buses and wanted to buy one for years, but his wife wouldn't agree. One day, I stopped by his office and, to my surprise, there was a bus parked behind his company [office]. He proudly told me he had finally realized his dream of owning a bus. When I asked about his wife's reaction, he said, 'She doesn't know yet!'"

Why do couples lie about money? You may think it is a result of greed, but it is more about insecurity and a desire to avoid conflict. Many people want their partners to think they are smart when it comes to money. When they make a financial mistake or spend money in a way that does not fit with their partner's value system, they would rather lie than talk about it. And while talking about it is a good idea, the fear is that if I am honest with my spouse, we are going to fight. (Refer to Myth 4.)

IN HIS OWN WORDS

I always round the price down so she won't get angry. If I buy some bike gear, I tell her it costs $150 if the actual price is $169. I figure that sounds better than $170. It's just a little white lie.
—*JAMISON, 53-YEAR-OLD MARRIED COMPUTER PROGRAMMER*

Avoiding money conflicts often leads to secrecy, which is unhealthy for a long-term relationship. Secrecy erodes trust, and when the truth is discovered, the effort to repair this breach may be too much for the already troubled relationship to endure. Financial secrecy is a form of infidelity in which one or both of the partners act in a way that goes against what the couple had previously decided about how to save, spend, or invest money. This type of money behavior often reflects a more serious marital concern. This may include an imbalance in power and control in the marriage, lack of respect for each other, or an inability to identify and resolve conflict. Although the deeper issues are not in your purview as an advisor, it is important to notice when these forces are at play. (Refer to Chapter 12, "Special Issues in Advising Couples," for ideas on how to make an effective couple and marital counseling referral.)

It is important to note that there is a difference between secrecy and privacy. Some financial privacy can be very healthy for a couple. For example, some couples decide, based on their money history, life experiences, and financial beliefs, to have two individual accounts in addition to their joint account, for each to use as he or she sees fit. This allows the partners to feel empowered and in control of their money, while at the same time working together to manage the household funds. In this situation, financial privacy is valued by the partners and exercised through the use of both "my" and "our" money.

Myth 4. Couples *always* fight about money. According to the American Institute of CPAs, 27 percent of married couples or couples living together fight about finances more than any other issue. The study reports that these disagreements occur on average three times a month and are often focused on unforeseen expenses such as a car repair, insufficient savings balances, or differing viewpoints on how the partners defined financial needs versus financial wants.[2] Although this statistic is concerning and is part of the reason couples need good financial advisors to work with, it suggests that all couples who talk about money fight about finances. Instead, many couples do just fine. And the others may just need training in how to have a money conversation from a couple-friendly advisor like you.

What about the 73 percent of couples who don't view money as the most contentious issue in their marriage or partnership? Do these partners know how to talk openly about finances, or do they engage in *money silence* to avoid conflict? Money silence is what happens when a couple has an unspoken agreement that says, "We will avoid directly discussing money and finance at all costs." In many instances, the pact is made because one or both of the partners came from a family where the parents fought about money. A person who grew up in this sort of household felt emotionally unsafe as a child and continues to carry highly charged memories. To escape repeating this pattern, the person vows to sidestep any and all money conversations with the intent of never feeling that unsafe again. This approach works for a while. However, when financial matters are not overtly discussed, problems remain unresolved, and resentment festers. In the end, the issues get bigger and bleed into other nonmonetary areas of the relationship. For some couples, this is the beginning of the end of a marriage. Others end up in your office looking for assistance.

Conflict is inevitable in any long-term relationship, but fighting is not. Some couples have the skills to calmly work through financial differences; others need some coaching to learn how to fight fair financially. As a financial advisor, you have a responsibility to educate your couple clients about the role of healthy conflict in their financial lives.

IN HIS OWN WORDS

I avoid money conversations, but when I'm honest with my wife and we talk about money more openly, I actually feel closer as opposed to further apart.

—MATT, 40-YEAR-OLD SOCIAL WORKER AND FATHER OF TWO

Myth 5. Couples should *always* agree financially. Similar to the myth about couples always fighting about money, there is a misconception that financial harmony means that a couple should always agree financially. This myth stems from our conflict-avoidant culture.

The belief is that conflict is bad and to be avoided at all costs; full agreement between parties is good and the best outcome. Not so fast—it is sometimes healthy to have diverse viewpoints when it comes to money and investments. This allows a couple to explore differences, learn from each other, and then together arrive at a solution that may be better than one offered by either member individually.

One of the biggest mistakes advisors make in coaching couples is to buy into the idea that two people have to agree on every part of their financial plan. The conversation gets misdirected toward identifying who is right and who is wrong. Instead, the objective needs to be assisting the partners in understanding and exploring both differences and commonalities. The question is, "How can I help each person understand the other's viewpoint?" From there, you can coach them to compromise and, if necessary, agree to disagree.

If couples always agreed financially, your job would be pretty boring. Spouses would have the same risk tolerance, desire the same portfolio mix, and always want to retire at the same age. There really would not be any demand for financial advisors, would there? But the truth is that couples need someone like you to facilitate a productive financial dialogue, as their opinions will differ from time to time. So don't work so hard to find the winner of a financial debate; instead, declare both partners victors and design a plan that capitalizes on the strengths and differences of each partner.

Myth 6. Women need to be rescued financially. As you can imagine, this is my least favorite couples and money myth, but it is pervasive in our culture. From almost the beginning of time, marriage was an economic contract that stated that the husband would provide monetarily for the wife, so long as the wife gave him children and took care of the home. It has only been in the last fifty years that women have made major economic progress and are now an equal economic force if not a greater one than men. Even so, the belief that women need to be rescued financially is still deeply woven into our societal fabric. Many young women joke that they don't need to save money now because a "spouse comes with a house" or a "man is a plan." In the early 1900s, this was true and was typically the only way for a woman to amass wealth. However, this truth is rapidly changing as the wage gap lessens and women make more money than ever before.

A 2010 study conducted by Reach Advisors determined that childless single women between the ages of 22 and 30 have a median income exceeding that of their male peers. Yes, women made more money than men for the first time in history! This trend is seen in large cities such as Atlanta, Memphis, Charlotte, New York, and Sacramento. The researchers hypothesized that these cities were postindustrial, knowledge-based economies, which attract a well-educated population and favored women, who currently earn 57 percent of all undergraduate degrees and the majority of doctorate and master's degrees.[3] Increasingly, women are becoming major contributors to the family income, and it is estimated that women are contributing nearly 50 percent to a family's income.[4] As more men lose jobs in the current economy, more women are stepping up to the plate to provide for the household. Almost 40 percent of wives in the United States now outearn their husbands.[5] These women don't need to be saved, they need to be celebrated. And many of them are rescuing their male partners during this economic downturn.

Although more women are financially independent in their 20s and early 30s and earning more than ever before, many remain financially unsure of themselves. In a 2007 study conducted by Ramit Sethi, a personal-finance blogger for the millennial generation and author of *I Will Teach You to Be Rich*, he found that 44 percent of the young women surveyed, compared to 58 percent of the young men, said that they felt "confident" about money and finances.[6] While this is an improvement from yesteryear, it is clear that women still need to work on their financial self-esteem. As you know, self-esteem can be raised only by the person who is struggling. Therefore, women cannot be saved through marriage, as the myth suggests. A woman needs to rescue herself, find her confidence, and continue to take an equal role in family finances.

IN HER OWN WORDS

Once I understood money, it changed so much for me. It changed how I felt about myself. I felt more powerful, confident, and self-sufficient.

—*MARIA, 49-YEAR-OLD MARRIED BUSINESS OWNER AND STEPMOTHER OF THREE*

Myth 7. Men are financially savvy; women are financially naïve.
I suspect there are just as many men who are not financially literate as there are women. But few men admit it, and therefore the myth continues that women are financially naïve and men are financially savvy. The reality is, many women are financially intelligent and are offended by advisors who assume their literacy based solely on their gender.

What accounts for the belief that men are born financially smart and women are not? Part of it is a long history of men being the wealth controllers and women being financially dependent on men, not because of their intelligence but because of social expectations and constraints. Although a thorough examination of all these factors is not within the realm of this book, it is worth noting that women have a complex history around money, as for centuries they were oppressed by men who controlled their economic destiny.

In addition, gender does influence how men and women display confidence and vulnerability when it comes to finances as well as life. From an early age, men are socialized to never admit weakness. If a man is meeting with you along with his wife, and he doesn't understand what you are saying, there is a high likelihood that he will not let on. His motivation is not deception but to save face in front of you and his wife. On the contrary, women are socialized from a young age to show vulnerabilities and admit (almost to a fault) when they are not good at something. Often female clients overstate their lack of knowledge, whereas men understate it. And some women, often from older generations, are financially savvy, but out of respect for their husbands, don't show this knowledge publicly.

No matter what the case is, gender does not determine a person's level of financial intelligence. To assume so jeopardizes the work you can do with couples and the alliance you have with each partner. Remember, women still statistically live longer than men, so make sure you don't fall into this trap if you want to retain widows.

The Advisor's Couples Mindset

As an advisor, you grew up in the same society as your clients; therefore, you have been influenced by many of the same couple and money myths as they have. You are also a product of your upbringing and the couple money messages that your parents instilled in you. Together these societal messages and your personal money beliefs make up your couples mindset. This mindset is not good or bad, but it is important to identify it when you are working with couple clients. By doing so, you are acknowledging your biases and any potential blind spots you may have when advising couples.

For example, Diana, a veteran in working with couples, notices that when two spouses come in and report that they have separate financial accounts, she flinches. Her automatic thought is, "There is something wrong with the trust and communication in this partnership." This thought or money script is based on how her parents and, subsequently, she and her husband manage money in their marriage. Her awareness of her couples mindset on joint accounts allows her to not react with judgment. Instead she becomes curious: "Over the years, I have learned that when I have a certain mindset about how couples should manage finances, I need to ask a lot of probing questions. This allows me to learn more about the two individuals in the room and how they have decided to manage money and make financial decisions together. It is easy to think my way is the best way, but it really is up to the couple and what works for them."

In Her Own Words

It is so important to have a beginner's mind when coaching couples on money.
—SHELL TAIN, 61-YEAR-OLD MARRIED OWNER OF SENSIBLE COACHING

There is no way to be a human being and not have preconceived notions as to how couples should act and not act around money. What is important is to identify these beliefs and be aware of how these thoughts could block you from understanding the couple in front of you. The bottom line is that there is no right way to manage money as a couple. Instead, a couple-friendly advisor opens his or her mind to the plethora of possibilities and remains a neutral facilitator. The goal is to assist the partners in figuring out what methods work best for them and their unique situation. This neutrality is not always easy to achieve, but it is vital to effectively advising couples.

Summary

The truth is, money is a complex and tricky part of a relationship. As an advisor, you see how complicated it can get for couples every day. Finances are often a stressor in marriage, and failure to communicate effectively around money is one of the main reasons for divorce. As a financial advisor, you can teach couples the myths about couples and money, and assist them in developing healthier, more well-balanced ideas about how love, money, and partnership truly work.

This requires you to put your preconceived notions aside too. What works for you may not work for them. The goal of a couple-friendly advisor is to be curious, to listen carefully to both partners' perspectives, to put your ideas of what is right aside, and to be a role model for what healthy, open-minded financial communication looks like.

Maybe if Cinderella had had a good financial advisor, she would not have needed Prince Charming to rescue her from poverty. Instead, she and her prince could have amassed wealth and managed the finances of the kingdom together.

Your Next Step: Identifying Your Couples Mindset

To further explore your thoughts and beliefs about couples and money, complete the following sentences. It is important to complete this exercise quickly and not to edit your initial responses. Remember, there are no right or wrong responses, just the ones that resonate with you.

1. Couples and money are _____

2. The perfect couple is _____

3. The most important lesson my parents taught me about couples and money is _____

4. My mother taught me that women in couples are _____
   _____

5. My father taught me that men in couples are _____
   _____

6. Men who control the family finances in a couple are _____
   _____

7. Women who control the family finances are _____
   _____

8. Couples who fight about money are _____
   _____

9. Couples who don't fight about money are _____

_____

10. If I entered a room with all the love I wanted on one side
    of the room, and all the money I wanted on the other side,
    I would _____

Now review your answers, noticing any themes in your responses. What did you discover? Do your beliefs about couplehood match with the type of couple clients you attract to your practice? Or are your beliefs out of sync with the type of couples you counsel? Now, write a sentence or two that summarizes your current couples mindset and then list three ways in which your couples mindset helps you in your practice and three ways in which it may hinder your work or present a potential blind spot.

My couples mindset is: _____

_____

This mindset helps me:

1. _____

2. _____

3. _____

This mindset may hinder me:

1. _____

2. _____

3. _____

3

Advising and Couple Dynamics

The meeting of two personalities is like the contact
of two chemical substances: If there is any reaction,
both are transformed.

—Carl Jung, founder of Jungian psychology

EARLY IN MY CAREER, I WOULD MEET WITH COUPLES AND ALWAYS
walk away thinking, "What a nice guy." My thoughts about the
women were less favorable. One day when consulting with a more
seasoned colleague, she asked me why I thought I always connected
with the men and felt disconnected with the women. A lightbulb
went on. Without realizing it, I was recreating my family dynamic.
When I was growing up, my dad and I were very close, which often
caused tension between my mother and me. It was easy and comfortable for me to play that role—too easy, it seems.

What I learned that day was vital to my work with couples
moving forward. I, like every professional, had blind spots when
working with clients. My responsibility was to both partners; therefore, I needed to be aware of the dynamics of the couple, and how
my family upbringing had the potential to cloud my perception.

Fortunately, I was working in a field that encouraged consultation. Otherwise, my work with these couples and families would not have been as effective.

In the financial services industry, identifying blind spots, including how an advisor's family history impacts the advising process, is not commonplace. It is seen as "soft" and not as valid as consultation regarding the technical aspects of finance. The result is that many well-meaning advisors fall into traps not because they are not competent, but because of their lack of training in the dynamics of couples and the psychology of money. The good news is that by reading this book, you are making a commitment to learn more about the psychology of financial planning. This knowledge will assist you in advising couples more effectively and avoiding the common pitfalls of this type of work. Not only will your meetings be more productive, but your financial solutions will be more creative and, ultimately, more successful.

Don't Fall for the Bait

There are several traps an advisor can fall into when working with couples. These traps are not intentionally set by your couple clients. In fact, they often have no awareness that these dynamics are part of their relationship. Your job is to notice when you may be falling into a trap and avoid it when possible. You do not need to explore why this dynamic exists in the couple, as that is the work of psychotherapy. But you do need to be cognizant of how a particular couple's dynamics impact the advisor–couple client relationship. In doing so, you will find your work with couples less frustrating and more satisfying.

Triangulation

When working with couples, you are involved in what the field of psychology calls *triangulation*. This simply means that you are in a three-person relationship system comprising you and the two members of the couple. The danger involved in being part of a triangular relationship is that it is easy to be caught in the middle of conflicts. The result is that the two people involved in the misunderstanding avoid directly addressing the underlying issues by conversing through you, instead of directly with each other.

For example, a husband attends an appointment alone and complains that his wife spends too much money and has a shopping problem. He is looking for you to agree with him. If you do, then he feels less anxious and does not have to confront his wife directly. He can talk about it with you and reduce his angst, but nothing changes. The real issue is more complex than what the husband presents. But the belief he has, and you need to be careful not to buy into, is that she just needs to stop spending money and everything will be fine. If you dig a little deeper, you may discover that he is tight with money and her spending is reasonable. Or maybe she shops to escape the loneliness she feels in the marriage. Whatever the root of the problem, you need to be careful to not get pulled into an unhealthy triangulation. In this situation, the best course of action is to invite her into a meeting with him and facilitate a dialogue between the two spouses about their different viewpoints regarding spending. In this role, you are an observer of the dynamic, not a participant. And if the couple is motivated to change, then the real work can begin.

Be careful not to unknowingly fall into taking on the role you did in your own family. One advisor I coached explained how being the oldest son in his family of origin resulted in his unconsciously siding with the less powerful member of the couple. On reflection, he realized that he was trying to protect the less dominant spouse similarly to how he would protect his younger siblings against bullies at school. By becoming aware of this tendency, he took steps to notice when he felt pulled to save one partner over the other and did not act on it. With this insight, he could advocate for both members of the couple to be heard and stay a neutral observer.

IN HIS OWN WORDS

Growing up, I was the peacekeeper in my family. Currently, I try very hard to keep my mother and my wife happy. The result is I end up miserable.

—RYAN, 58-YEAR-OLD MARRIED ENTREPRENEUR AND FATHER OF THREE

There is no way to avoid a triangular relationship with a couple. It is rare that advisors work in offices that are large enough for two advisors to attend every couple meeting. While this can mitigate the potential for triangulation, it is impractical in most circumstances. Therefore, you need to become adept at identifying when this couple dynamic occurs and develop strategies for counteracting it. The first step is being aware of the concept of triangulation and how you might be pulled into taking sides. In later chapters, you will learn specific strategies for remaining neutral even when couples want you to place blame.

Projection

How many times have you met with a client and thought, "This client is so like me."? Chances are you enjoyed the person and may even have attributed your own experiences to him. This is called *projection*, which means you have taken your own feelings and ascribed them to someone else. The problem with this tendency is that you are not your client. His or her experience may be similar to yours, or it could be vastly different. If you project and overidentify with one member of a couple, you might find yourself acting in ways that are not helpful for both members of the partnership.

For example, a couple in their late forties comes to you for financial planning. The wife is worried about saving money for retirement and is clearly annoyed with her husband, who does not share her same urgency. As you sit and listen to them tell their story, your mind wanders off to a recent discussion you had with your significant other. You know exactly how this woman feels—unheard and unloved. This data is unrelated to this couple and their retirement dilemma, but you project your feelings onto the wife. When they ask for your professional opinion, you tell the husband that he needs to listen more to his wife and start taking retirement savings more seriously. On the surface, this seems like a sound recommendation. You have validated the wife's feelings, and you know that a higher balance in a retirement account is more often than not a good thing. But what you have failed to do is understand the husband's perspective. What are his feelings about retirement? What causes him to not worry about this next phase of his life? How might his lack of concern be fueling her need to worry more? By projecting your own thoughts, feelings, and beliefs onto this couple's situation, you lost your curiosity. You did not get all the facts before making your recommendation. Time will tell if this advice was helpful. At best, they will be back in your office having the same argument. At worst, the husband will fire you and move on to an advisor who takes the time to understand his position too.

In Her Own Words

You need to remind yourself to check your preconceived notions at the door. Some women do care about beating the benchmarks and some men leave the finances to the wife. You don't know until you get inside the dynamic of that particular couple.
—KELLY SHIKANY, CFP, VOGELSANG ASSET MANAGEMENT

Remember that there are three sides to every story—his version, her version, and the truth. When you fall into the trap of projection, you miss out on important data about the couple that may alter the advice you give. So the next time you like a client or think you understand the person, stop yourself. Get curious and remember that everyone's experience in life is unique to him or her.

Personalization

Working with couples and helping them change their financial habits can stir up emotions for both clients and advisors. If you have done this work for a while, you know clients can talk and act in ways ranging from annoying to downright infuriating. Although it is important that you recognize and eventually process your reaction, it is paramount that you separate your personal feelings from what is going on with the couple during the meeting.

It is easy to fall into the trap of defending yourself in meetings, especially when a client expresses anger at you. Instead of reacting, take a deep breath and refocus your energy on understanding what this is about for the person or the couple. Your job is not to make everyone happy and tie up all financial conflicts with a big red bow. Instead, you are tasked with translating what each partner is saying about a particular issue and labeling areas of commonality and difference. Sometimes this means being the bad guy temporarily for the best interests of the couple in the long run.

Being able to manage your emotional reactions during meetings is part of a skill called *advisor self-management*. Self-management involves noticing thoughts and feelings that arise in your client work but not acting on them. Often what is getting stirred up inside you is not useful to share with the couple. Even if it is, the time to share your thoughts would be after you have calmed down and can rationally understand what is going on for you in the advisor–client relationship.

The best way to handle a hostile client is to get curious. Ask open-ended questions as a way of refocusing the conversation on the clients and their concerns. Keep in mind that when people get scared, they often use anger to feel more in control. Therefore, if you empathize with the situation and the client's pain, not only does this help you stay in the room for the rest of the meeting, but it calms the client down too.

Advising couples sometimes means experiencing uncomfortable feelings and being the target of negative emotions. As a couple-friendly professional, know that this is part of the process and remember, like it or not, it usually is not about you.

The Five Tenets of Couple Dynamics

Advising couples effectively requires an understanding of the basic truths about how couples operate and interact. Although there is a lot more to know about family systems and couple dynamics, the following five tenets can give you some insight into why couples act the way they do inside your office.

Tenet 1: Money Is a Reflection of the Couple Dynamic

Money is much more than a tool for trading goods and services. It symbolizes power, control, commitment, confidence, freedom, love, trust, self-worth, and security. How money is managed in a couple is a reflection of how they interact and operate together and with the world around them. For example, a couple who maintain joint accounts and make financial decisions collaboratively, most likely trust each other and believe in equality in the relationship. Conversely, couples who maintain separate accounts despite being in a long-term committed relationship communicate their values of autonomy and independence. Neither approach is right or wrong, but each does give you some insight into the couple's dynamic.

In addition to how couples manage money, how the partners spend money also mirrors their values and points to their potential areas of disagreement. For example, a husband who insists on driving a Mercedes even though the couple has high credit card debt is clearly saying he values status more than security. If his wife is secretly stashing money away in an undisclosed account, she is communicating her need for safety and independence. The fact that there is a financial secret in their relationship begs the question, "In what other areas do they withhold information from each other?" While secret keeping is more common than you would think in relationships, it can be a form of betrayal that erode trust.

As an advisor, you are tasked with helping couples articulate their values and how their money behaviors reflect these ideals. When there is a disconnect between a person's beliefs and behaviors and his or her partner's, it's best to explore this disconnect. The goal is to assist couples in understanding each other's position and how these common or varying beliefs serve or do not serve the couple financially. As Margaret Shapiro, a family therapist specializing in money issues, states, "A financial portfolio must also include an emotional portfolio. Both portfolios need careful attention and management for risk and growth."[1]

Tenet 2: Couples Crave Balance

Homeostasis is a concept taught in middle school science class that refers to organisms' desire to live in equilibrium. Just like any other living organism, a couple works to keep its system in balance. You have probably noticed this in your own practice. Think about how many savers are married to spenders. This is a great way for a couple to stay balanced. If the spender decides to decrease his cash outflow, then watch out for the saver to start spending more. Often this rebalancing is not conscious on the part of the couple.

Couples unconsciously keeping the couple system in balance can make your job frustrating. At times the partners will make promises and intend to change money habits, only to end up with each person shifting just enough for the couple to stay the same. Noticing this tendency can be helpful in facilitating change. It brings the behaviors to conscious thought, which makes it easier for the couple to act differently going forward. This type of noticing is not a guarantee of behavioral change, but it does pave the way for the possibility of new ways of interacting with money together.

A couple's natural tendency to gravitate toward homeostasis highlights why it is vital to have both partners present for the meetings and planning sessions. Real change is only going to occur in a couple when both members are willing and motivated to do something different. If one partner is left out of the dialogue, it is hard to know if the couple as a system is on board with the plan.

This tenet also helps in reducing your frustration level. There are couples who remain stuck in their dynamic no matter what good financial advice they receive. In these instances, let go of trying to save the couple and instead focus your energy on clients who are motivated and willing to engage in the uncomfortable work of changing.

Tenet 3: Opposites Attract, Then Repel

The saying "opposites attract" is often true when it comes to couples and money. Spenders marry savers. Investment junkies marry financial avoiders. Analytic types marry feeling types. The list goes on. At first, these polarized viewpoints draw a couple together. A spender loves and admires his partner's help in saving some of their income. A financial avoider is relieved that she no longer has to feel guilty because she is not interested or proactive in investing her money. The analytic loves the spontaneity of a more feeling-oriented partner. However, as time progresses and love matures, these appealing traits morph into habits that repel, or at least annoy, the partners.

Karen is a 43-year-old paralegal who has been married for 10 years to Dan, a 41-year-old mechanical engineer. She loves a bargain but can also splurge on fine wine and expensive meals. Her husband sees a meal as nutrition, not entertainment, and prefers not to waste money dining out. As Karen put it in our interview, "What attracted me to Dan was he can get blood from a stone and is extremely disciplined with money. It is now the thing that sometimes drives me crazy!"

Even when couples are both on the saving side or the spending side of the spectrum, you see them differentiate along a continuum. Two people who are thrifty will split into one who is a super saver and one who saves from time to time. The reason for this polarization is that couples, like all systems, like to maintain equilibrium, and this helps them do so.

In His Own Words

All my spontaneous purchases are planned well in advance.
—*Dan, 41-year-old married mechanical engineer and father of one*

In a healthy couple, the individuals grow and mature over time and meet somewhere in the middle. For example, when I married my husband, Brian, he was a spender. He did not have a lot of money, but he certainly enjoyed spontaneously spending it on himself and others. I, being an FDIC bank examiner at the time, was the consummate saver. I firmly believed that spending should be planned, and that any and all impulsive spending was irresponsible. Over time, we each loosened up and found ways to appreciate and adopt some of the other person's money personality. My husband learned to save and plan more and is often the one to utter, "Can we afford this right now?" I discovered that joy can come from a spontaneous expense and that it is a problem only if you always spend money this way. Together we balance each other out without having to hang onto such polarized views about money.

Your goal in advising couples is not to convince one member to adopt the other person's viewpoint. Instead, you want to encourage the couple to select the best attributes from each person's money personality so they can optimize their family's financial health now and for many years to come.

Tenet 4: Couples Repeat Family Patterns

The psychological term for this phenomenon is *repetition compulsion*. This is a fancy way of saying that people repeat the interpersonal and communication patterns of their ancestors. This is why the last time you scolded your son, you said to your wife, "Oh, goodness, I sound like my dad." You did; you repeated a pattern that you witnessed growing up and are now modeling this behavior to your children, who most likely will carry on the tradition. Before you get too worked up about this concept, know that sometimes people do the exact opposite of what they learned from their family of origin. For example, if your wife grew up with parents who yelled at each other, she may avoid conflicts and rarely raise her voice to you. As an adult, you probably mimic quite a few of your family's behaviors, but have also left some behind.

Family patterns show up in the advising session as thoughts and beliefs about money and its purpose in the world. A couple may be discussing whether or not to buy their son a car for his sixteenth birthday. Both of them have an argument for why the son should or should not get this gift. When asked about their personal experiences turning 16 and what gifts they received, you learn that the father, who is in favor of buying the car, came from an affluent family where giving a 16-year-old a car was a longstanding tradition. The wife, who grew up in a much more modest home, would never have dreamed of asking for or receiving such a lavish gift at 16 years of age. Both spouses have valid perspectives derived from their family upbringing. Your work is to help them each voice their thoughts and find a solution that is agreeable to both. For example, maybe the couple can put a sizable down payment on the car and let the son pay off the remainder of the loan over time. The husband can honor his family tradition, while his wife can teach her son the value of money.

When you see two people sitting in front of you during a meeting, remember that they are surrounded by their ancestors' money messages. Appreciate these voices from the past and assist clients in identifying how these historical money attitudes influence their financial decisions today. Unless clients have a chance to consciously examine these family money messages, patterns will be repeated. In Part II, "Essential Skills for Couple-Friendly Advisors," you will learn techniques for uncovering these messages.

Tenet 5: Couples Use Money to Vie for Power and Control

Every time my husband and I drive to Vermont, we have the same argument. I am driving in traffic, and he tells me what lane to drive in, when to speed up, and when to slow down. Needless to say, it makes me nuts! When I tell him I am a capable driver, he replies, "I am just helping." I retort, "I don't want or need your help." And then he utters, "Sorry." We must engage in this same verbal exchange 100 times a year, which proves that even experts become victims of the couple dynamics they teach. What this argument is really about is who is in control. Is it the person who is driving? Is it the person giving the commands? Who? I have to tell you, when it comes to driving to Vermont, we are still trying to figure that one out!

If you have ever driven in a car with your significant other, chances are you can identify with this story. The reason is that all couples vie for power and control in the relationship. It is just part of couplehood. This issue arises when discussing how to raise the kids, what family to visit for the holidays, or how to invest the family's assets. If you think about it, couples spend their entire lives negotiating power and control.

Money is often used to establish power and maintain control in a relationship. Therefore, this dynamic plays out in your office frequently. Consider the husband who wants his wife to write down every expense she incurs throughout the day. Although he may not realize it, this type of reporting makes him feel better and her worse. Eventually, she may rebel and act out financially. The wife starts to omit expenses from the list or loses the piece of paper on which she wrote the information. Both are attempts to regain control over her money. Unless this couple identifies how this reporting works and does not work for them, both partners are likely to exert their power in destructive ways.

There are many ways in which this dynamic shows up in your office. There is the wife who complains that she has to manage all the finances, but declines to let her husband take over the check-book for a month. There is the boyfriend who takes his girlfriend's credit cards away in an attempt to stop her from running up more debt. And there are the partners who argue for months on end if they are going to get a new living room set or go on a weekend trip to Aruba.

The truth is, we all like to feel powerful and in control. How we accomplish this as it relates to money varies according to our money personality, our family history, and our insight into our behavior. In a healthy relationship, both partners have input into how their money will be managed and if the authority is shared or delegated. Therefore, a power imbalance in a partnership is fine as long as both members of the couple agree with it. It is when one member feels overly regulated financially that conflict occurs. One woman put it this way, "He controls all the money. He even calls it *his money*. It is insulting and makes me feel worthless." Although this was not her husband's intent, it certainly was the result of his micromanagement of her spending. Eventually they looked at their family money histories and discovered how this agreement had been unconsciously set up early in their relationship. Together, they decided on a new system that empowered both of them to feel in control and worthwhile.

Two Can Tango

When conflict arises, it is important to keep in mind that each partner is part of the problem and part of the solution. Often couples want you to declare who is the victim and who is the victimizer. But, two can tango and often play both roles simultaneously.

IN HER OWN WORDS

I always complained to my husband that he didn't pay the bills and got to remain a financial adolescent in our relationship. Then one day, we sat down together to pay bills and balance the checkbook and I almost had a panic attack. It was then I realized I was part of the problem too.

—*MICHAELA, 55-YEAR-OLD MARRIED SCHOOLTEACHER*

For example, the husband who wants his wife to report every penny she spends is treating her like a child, and therefore is a victimizer. However, he also is a victim of her financial infidelities. Conversely, the wife is a victim of her husband's scrutiny but is victimizing him by not being up front about her resentment. To change this unhealthy pattern, both partners will have to be honest about their feelings and roles in perpetuating the situation. Often this is where couples get stuck and need a skilled advisor like you to help them achieve resolution. They need to be reassured that changing money patterns can initially be uncomfortable. However, with time and practice, the new behavior will eventually become second nature. What many couples need is for you to hold their proverbial hand during this phase. It is a valuable service and one that breeds trust and loyalty. The five tenets of couple dynamics give you some insight into how and why partners interact and communicate about money and investments the way they do. If you take the time to understand the softer side of finance with your couple clients, you will be better equipped to make concrete financial recommendations that stick.

Couples and Culture

When working with couples, it is important to consider the culture they were raised in and how spirituality may impact their view of wealth. While the tenets of couple dynamics remain valid, you must view them through the appropriate cultural lens. What may appear as controlling behavior in one culture is the status quo in another. For example, in Latino cultures, machismo is a cultural norm. You may see the husband's actions toward his wife as sexist and narrow-minded, but these behaviors may be more reflective of cultural expectations than issues of power and control in the relationship. In Japan, constant eye contact is considered rude. You may misread a wife's inconsistent eye contact as a lack of self-confidence or a disinterest in finance, when she may be just trying to be polite.

When working with couples from a diverse cultural or religious background, take the time to learn about their life experience and societal norms. Ask open-ended questions and find out more about the traditions and principles practiced relative to marriage and family life. Keep an open mind and make sure you put their interactions into a cultural context.

Summary

In this chapter, you learned about the common traps advisors fall into when coaching couples. You discovered how to start avoiding these pitfalls by increasing your understanding of human psychology and couple dynamics. The five tenets of couple dynamics were reviewed, along with some tips on how to recognize when these forces are at play in your office.

Remember to always view couple interactions through a culture lens, and when in doubt, ask curious questions to learn more about their money history and cultural background. Consider taking the initiative to acquire more education and training on couple dynamics. Not only will your work with couples greatly improve, but this will distinguish you and your services from the competition.

Your Next Step: Couple Dynamics Audit

Identifying and working with the dynamics of couples in your advisor–client relationships takes practice. To start this learning process, select two couples you currently advise and perform a couple dynamics audit. Later on you can run more couples through this process, but for now let's keep it simple. Select one couple you enjoy working with and call these clients your "ideal couple." Next, pick one couple you find difficult or frustrating to work with and label these clients your "nightmare couple." My guess is that your nightmare couple was easier to identify, as these types of clients are often hard to forget. Now fill in the couple dynamics chart.

Couple Dynamics Audit		
	Couple 1: *Ideal*	**Couple 2:** *Nightmare*
1. How are financial decisions made?	Example: *Jointly*	
2. How are the couple's accounts held?	*Jointly*	
3. Who is dominant in the meetings?	*Both*	
4. What is the tone of the meetings?	*Calm*	
5. How does this couple balance each other out?	*He is a spender/ She saves*	
6. What do I notice about me when meeting with Partner 1?	*I like him*	

7. What do I notice about me when meeting with Partner 2?	*She reminds me of my mom*	
8. What do I notice when I meet with the couple jointly?	*They work as a team*	
9. How might my reactions be part of my family history?	*My parents were a financial team*	
10. What thoughts and feelings might I project onto the couple?	*That they never fight about money*	
11. Which partner do I tend to want to side with when there is disagreement?	*Husband*	
12. What makes me most angry working with this couple?	*When he doesn't defend himself*	
13. What makes me most joyful when working with this couple?	*When we laugh*	
14. What culture(s) are the partners from and how does this impact the dynamic?	*Irish Catholic; might have conflicts about wealth based on idealism of poor*	
15. What else do I notice about the couple's dynamics?	*It feels familiar*	

Now review both columns, noticing any trends. What resonates with or goes against your beliefs about couples and money? How might these attitudes trigger you in an advising session? Now capture this data below:

My ideal couple client is defined as: _____

_____

This type of client taps into my family history by: _____

_____

I must be careful not to fall into the following traps when working with this couple: _____

_____

My nightmare couple client is defined as: _____

_____

This type of client taps into my family history because: _____

_____

I must be careful not to fall into the following traps when working with this couple: _____

_____

Over time, use this couple dynamics audit with all your couple clients. If this is a large number, then complete this audit as part of your preparation for each couple's annual meeting. This way the information is fresh in your mind for the meeting. As you become more skilled at recognizing and working with couple dynamics, you can update the data accordingly.

—————————————●（4）●—————————————

The Modern Couple

Most people assume that women are responsible
for households and child care. . . . Most couples
operate that way—not all. That fundamental
assumption holds women back.

—Sheryl Sandberg, COO, Facebook

ONE OF MY FAVORITE TELEVISION SHOWS IS THE EMMY AWARD–
winning *Modern Family*. Besides being well-written and hilarious,
it speaks to how the definition of couples and families has changed
over the past decade. The cast of characters includes Claire and Phil,
the traditional family rearing three school-aged children; Mitchell
and Cameron, a married gay couple with an adopted daughter;
and Jay, Claire and Mitchell's dad, and his second wife, Gloria, a
blended family rearing Gloria's son from her first marriage and their
own newborn. As you can imagine, the hijinks that ensue are a belly
laugh a minute.

Popular culture tends to mirror current themes, and it signals
shifts in societal rules. Think back to *The Dick Van Dyke Show*,
which first aired in 1961. This show celebrated the traditional all-
American family unit with Rob, the hard-working comedy writer;
Laura, his beautiful stay-at-home wife; and Ritchie, their son. All

of Rob and Laura Petrie's friends look a lot like them, and the comedy came from innocent misunderstandings between husband and wife.

This image of the American family radically changed in 1971 with the airing of the television show *All in the Family*. Archie Bunker, the main character, was a loudmouthed bigot who lived under one roof with his subservient wife, Edith; his daughter, Gloria; and her liberal, economically dependent husband, Michael. Archie was powerless to fight the ethnic and cultural changes in his neighborhood and the world. While he never accepted his college-educated son-in-law as a real man, he eventually befriended Lionel, the son of his black neighbor and adversary George Jefferson.

Around the same time, television series such as *The Brady Bunch* and *The Partridge Family* were teaching us about blended and single-parent families. Mike and Carol Brady were poster parents for second marriage as they raised each other's children, and Shirley Jones was a hip widow with five children touring the country as a rock-and-roll band. The definition of family was becoming more diverse, and our television sets were the windows into a larger, more complicated world.

In 1975, *The Jeffersons*, a spin-off from *All in the Family*, piloted. The show featured the financially upwardly mobile African American family and their cross-racial married friends. At the time, being a nonwhite business owner accumulating wealth and marrying someone of a different race were controversial topics. It spoke to the transformation occurring in society as a result of the Civil Rights Movement. *The Jeffersons* caught on, signaling that the world was ready for a new definition of family, marriage, and success.

Flash forward to 2009, when *Modern Family* debuted on ABC television. It was a radical concept: an extended family comprised of a potpourri of people from different ethnic backgrounds, generations, and sexual orientations living together as a typical American family. Once again the definition of couplehood and family was shifting, and the media was going to show us the way.

Since television sets found their way into our living rooms, the definition of couplehood and family has changed radically. In 1950, 43 percent of American homes were traditional in nature, meaning that they consisted of two married heterosexual partners and their respective children. Currently, this number is only 20 percent.[1] No longer the majority, traditional couples are being outnumbered by nontraditional partnerships, or what I like to call "modern couples." Modern couples are defined as those consisting of same-sex partners, unmarried couples living together, couples who decide not to have children, and blended families. The increase in these nontraditional unions is partially the result of more people opting to live together. In fact, from 1960 to 2010, the number of couples cohabiting increased 17-fold.[2] Other contributors include the feminist movement making it more routine for women to be financially equal to their partners, if not the primary breadwinners, and the gay rights movement making same-sex unions more commonplace.

As an advisor in a constantly changing world, you need to recognize how the definition of the modern couple has changed and may continue to morph as societal norms continue to evolve. Your couple clients are likely to include traditional couples similar to Rob and Laura Petrie as well as same-sex couples like Mitchell and Cameron. This diversity makes your job more interesting and more complicated. You need to be aware of the legal and financial aspects of different types of unions. You also need to be educated about how the psychological dynamics of each couple may vary according to their ages, backgrounds, and lifestyles. A couple-friendly advisor is both skilled in the technical aspects of financial planning, and open and willing to learn more about how the partners in front of them make, manage, and invest money. It is a whole new world, and the modern couple is here to stay.

Changing Demographics

Forty-eight percent of American households are made up of married couples, with only 20 percent of these homes being traditional in nature.[3] The remaining households are nontraditional by definition, with many couples opting to cohabit as opposed to legally marry. For couples who do tie the knot, they are walking down the aisle later in life. The median age of those married for the first time is now 28.3 for men and 25.8 for women.[4] This represents a jump in median age by approximately five years for both sexes since 1960.[5] Of those marriages, 40 to 50 percent end in divorce.[6] However, the percentage of couples who divorce dramatically decreases if the partners are reasonably well educated, make a decent living, are religious, married after 25 years of age and before having any children, and come from an intact family of origin.[7]

In addition to the changing demographic of couplehood, there is a trend toward women controlling more of the wealth in this country. Currently, women control the majority of personal wealth in the United States at 51.3 percent.[8] Those assets amount to more than $8 trillion and are expected to increase to $22 trillion by 2020.[9] Furthermore, women will inherit 70 percent of the $41 trillion in intergenerational wealth transfers due to occur over the next several decades, totaling approximately $28.7 trillion in assets.[10] Many of these women will become double inheritors, inheriting money from both parents and spouses. Others will accumulate wealth through their own professional and business accomplishments. In fact, women-owned businesses are growing at twice the national rate and account for 40 percent of privately held entities.[11,12] This growth is so rapid that one recent report by the Center for Women's Business Research claimed that "If U.S.-based women-owned businesses were their own country, they would have the fifth largest GDP in the world."[13] These statistics make a strong argument for why women need to be included when it comes to advising couples. They not only are an important part of a couple's financial life, but might just be the partners with the majority of the assets.

With modern couples, you can no longer assume that the partners who walk through your office door are traditional in nature. More often than not, the couples you advise will be diverse in age, lifestyle, and sexual orientation. This makes your job more interesting and more challenging. But it also makes the services of couple-friendly advisors more in demand. Couples no longer can fall back on clearly defined marital or gender roles. Instead, they need your assistance in discussing and figuring out how to manage money under this new, shifting paradigm of couplehood.

A New Division of Labor

In the thought-provoking book *The End of Men: And the Rise of Women*, the author Hanna Rosin introduces the concept of the "seesaw marriage." This is a partnership in which women are no longer dependent on men to provide for them financially. She states, "The new model of elite marriage renders even that simple equation obsolete. The prevailing arrangement now is a constantly shifting equation—sixty-forty or eighty-twenty or ninety-ten . . . where any side of that ratio can be filled by either partner at any given time."[14] What Rosin is referring to is the fact that gender roles in marriage have become less rigid, especially among the educated class. More women are becoming the primary breadwinners, and more dads are staying at home to raise the children. The expectation is that each couple gets to make financial and household decisions as a team, without strict societal constraints on what it means to be a husband/father versus a wife/mother.

Interestingly enough, female breadwinners have a tendency to share financial power with their male partners as opposed to ruling the roost as men who are primary earners tend to do. This may be because of the female preference for collaborative decision making, or it could be a result of a generational shift, as this tendency varies according to the age. For example, 71 percent of couples between the ages of 35 and 44, who are members of either generation Y or generation X, report that they manage money together. Only 13 percent of this age group reports the primary breadwinner managing money alone. For couples 65 years of age and older, who are either members of the first wave of baby boomers or traditionalists, 55 percent report sharing financial responsibilities and 28 percent report that the primary earner takes the lead.[15] You can't assume that gender roles in a financial meeting are just flipped when the woman is the primary earner. It is more complex and individualized than ever before.

The best course of action is to ask the couple sitting in your office open-ended questions to discern exactly how they make financial decisions, who earns the money, and how their respective incomes impact the financial planning process. The modern couple has more freedom when it comes to making and managing money; therefore, it is dangerous to make assumptions about who is the wealth creator and who oversees the household finances. Instead, start every client engagement with a beginner's mind and ask a series of questions to discover who does what in the partnership. Here are 10 questions to consider:[16]

1. How do you manage your money as a couple?
2. Do you each have access to separate money sources, or is it all combined?
3. What contributed to the decision to manage your money this way?
4. How do you make spending decisions as a couple?
5. How do you make investment decisions as a couple?
6. How do you make charitable-giving decisions as a couple?
7. How did you handle money when you were single? How has that changed now that you are in a partnership?
8. How often do you engage in money conversations as a couple? What is the typical tone of these conversations?
9. What happens if you don't agree on a financial decision?
10. Is there anything else you think is important for me to know about how you operate as a couple when it comes to money?

These inquiries help provide an accurate picture of how the couple operates financially and make sure you leave your assumptions at the door. Remember to revisit these questions periodically, as modern couples redefine tasks and responsibilities as their needs and priorities change. With the new seesaw marriage as the norm, it is vital to assess your couple clients where they are currently, and then adjust your understanding of them as they shift and morph over time.

Same-Sex Couples

With increased acceptance, more gay couples are seeking the counsel of financial advisors to help them navigate the complex legal and financial landscape of being in a same-sex partnership. This represents a challenge and an opportunity for you as an advisor. Some in the financial industry argue that only specialists should work with same-sex couples, but I don't agree. Often what it takes is an understanding of the historical context of these relationships along with a curiosity and acceptance of diversity. If you want to serve same-sex couples effectively, you need a willingness to learn and stay up to speed with the ever-changing legal aspects of gay marriage and domestic partnership, and remain open to these nontraditional lifestyles.

A Bit of Historical Context

It is unfortunate but true that historically, gay people have been viewed by society as outcasts. For generations, they have been prosecuted as criminals and seen as moral degenerates. Their sexual orientation has been labeled as mental illness and pathologized by leaders in the medical and psychiatric field. As a result, gay couples, until more recently, hid their sexual orientation from family and friends and relied only on each other for support. It was up to the couple to make the relationship work and figure out the financial aspects of the partnership. The thought of consulting with a financial services professional as a couple was seldom considered.

In the 1970s, the feminist movement revolutionized the gay experience. Same-sex couples started to develop safe communities where they found support and acceptance of their definition of family. There were still no legal safeguards for a same-sex couple; therefore, many still feared coming out publicly, as they risked losing jobs and children and alienating their family of origin. During the next two decades, progress was made in certain areas but lost in others. In 1986, "homosexuality" was removed as a mental disorder in the *Diagnostic and Statistical Manual of Mental Disorders: Third edition, Revised (DSM-III-R)*. The *DSM-III-R* is the bible for those working in the mental health profession and is used to determine the appropriate treatment for a client.[17] Removal from the *DSM-III-R* indicated more acceptance of same-sex partnerships by professionals in medicine and psychiatry.

A decade later, in 1996, the federal government enacted the Defense of Marriage Act (DOMA). This act explicitly rejects federal recognition of same-sex marriages and allows each state to refuse to recognize same-sex marriages performed in other states.[18] Around the same time, the Don't Ask, Don't Tell policy, which didn't ban gays from serving in the military, but required these individuals to keep their sexual orientation a secret, was adopted. Society in the 1980s and 1990s was sending mixed messages to same-sex couples.

In 2000 the tide turned when the governor of Vermont signed landmark legislation making the state the first in the country to grant the full benefits of marriage to same-sex couples. Although legal battles had been fought since the 1980s, this marked the real beginning of legal protection for gay couples. "Since 2000 there has been an absolute sea-change in the formalized recognition of the family," states Suzanne Slater, author of the *Lesbian Family Life Cycle* and founder of Gifted Generations. "We are more able to rely on limited formal recognition by major social institutions, and these improvements are more often now solidified by actual legal protections."[19] These laws allow some couples living in certain geographic locations to enjoy joint financial status, to benefit from family healthcare plans, and to have and maintain the custody of children. Although there is still more work to be done in this area, the trend is toward more states following Vermont's lead. There are now 13 states that have legalized same-sex marriage: California, Connecticut, Delaware, Iowa, Maine, Maryland, Massachusetts, Minnesota, New Hampshire, New York, Rhode Island, Vermont, and Washington as well as the District of Columbia. New Mexico recognizes same-sex marriages performed in other jurisdictions, and seven other states now offer broad protections short of marriage. These include Colorado, Hawaii, Illinois, and New Jersey, which allow civil unions; Oregon and Nevada, which offer broad domestic partnership; and Wisconsin, which has more limited domestic partnership. With these advances, a record number of Americans live in states that recognize relationships between same-sex couples.[20]

In the last 30 years there has been an unprecedented shift in how same-sex couples are perceived from both a legal and a social perspective. In June 2013, the Supreme Court overturned Section 3 of DOMA, making federal recognition of same-sex marriage mandatory.[21] However, the waters are still murky as this ruling does not require states that do not acknowledge gay marriages to do so. Therefore, a same-sex couples married in one of the 13 states that recognizes gay marriage will have full state and federal recognition as do heterosexual married couples in their state. But same-sex couples in the other states will not. Clearly, these couples need a knowledgeable and trustworthy advisor to help them navigate these turbulent waters and help them create the best possible financial plans for the future.

Advising Gay Couples

While a full discussion of all the ins and outs of same-sex financial planning is not within the scope of this book, it is important to be aware of the most common legal and financial issues that gay couples face. These include the complexities of starting a family, the lack of protection if a couple decides to divorce, and estate planning issues should one partner become ill and die. Let's look at each briefly.

Baby Makes Three

When it comes to starting a family, there are many legal and financial challenges to conquer. In their minds, both partners are parents of their new child, but this viewpoint is not necessarily shared by the law. In states where same-sex marriage is legal, it is easier to sort these issues out. Amy, a 39-year-old registered nurse married to Lori for seven years, explained her situation.

> *We are lucky to live in Massachusetts, where our marriage is legally recognized. When Lori and I made the decision to start a family, we met with an attorney to have wills, POAs, and healthcare proxies drawn up. We decided that Lori would be the one to carry our child because she is older than me, and at the time, I was also being treated for a chronic heart condition that would have made a pregnancy risky for me. After Lori got pregnant, we went back to our attorney to discuss the process for my adopting our unborn child, and we learned that there is a law in Massachusetts that states that if a woman is married at the time she gives birth, the person she is married to is automatically considered the father of the child, regardless of whether that person is the actual father or not. Fortunately, when the court legalized same-sex marriage, this statute remained in effect. Therefore, our attorney advised us to get married before the baby was born. Once we did that, all we needed to do was present our marriage certificate to the hospital registrar, and the birth certificate would list me as the second parent. We were one of the first couples in Massachusetts to test the law.*

Amy's story speaks to the progress some states have made in recognizing and providing some parity of benefits for same-sex parents. However, in the many states where same-sex marriage is not legal, questions regarding parental rights and responsibilities abound. It is important in your work with these couples that you collaborate with an attorney in your jurisdiction who can make sure the couple has the appropriate documents in place to protect their parental rights. These include at a minimum powers of attorney (POAs), detailed wills and estate planning documents, healthcare proxies, and domestic partnership agreements. These documents should be reviewed annually, as the laws and regulations relative to gay marriage continue to change.

Breaking Up Is Hard to Do

Now that more gay couples are getting married, there is more gay divorce. Unlike heterosexual couples, these individuals face big tax implications when they decide to split up. Because the federal government historically did not recognize gay marriage as legally valid, any transfer of assets between partners as part of divorce proceedings was viewed by the Internal Revenue Service as a "gift" and taxed accordingly.[22] Therefore, it was up to the couple to anticipate and financially plan for the dissolution of their union in order to not face substantial tax implications. With the recent overturn of DOMA, time will tell if this burden is lifted or just complicated by the disconnection between federal and individual state laws. As with most couples in love, asking partners to consider divorce when they are happy and satisfied with the relationship is a tricky and sometimes an impossible task. Gay couples are wise to draw up specific domestic partnership agreements, but are burdened by the additional legal expenses not incurred by more traditional couples. Furthermore, many couples are reluctant to take this action because of the real or anticipated emotional turmoil it may cause.

When any couple splits, the reaction of their families can range from openness and inclusion to negativity and exclusion. However, with a same-sex couple, the reaction of the family can have real legal and financial consequences. Will the grandparents exclude the children from a gay relationship from financial distributions because of the lack of biological or legal ties to the family? What about the ex-partner—will he or she be cut off too? According to Slater, "If there are grandkids, especially if they are biologically or legally tied only to the now-departing spouse, recognition of those kinship ties is completely dependent on the choices of the surrounding family, in terms of both continuing the relationship and also continuing financial gifts to the grandkids."[23] When a heterosexual marriage dissolves, there are laws and guidelines to protect the children, but there are no such protections when a same-sex partnership ends. For this reason, it is important to ask gay couples about how their respective families view their union. These questions include:

- How "out" are you with your family of origin?
- How do your family members, especially your parents, view your lifestyle?
- How might your family's feelings about your sexual orientation and this relationship impact your current or future children should you two split up?

By discussing these issues up front, you, as the advisor, and your clients will be better prepared if this unfortunate event occurs.

Till Death Do Us Part

When one member of a gay couple dies, there are no givens when it comes to inheriting the deceased partner's assets. Not only can surviving spouses be left with little, if anything, financially, but if they do receive money, they face costly tax consequences. Therefore, it is important to educate same-sex clients about these risks. The two biggest concerns relative to estate planning are taxation of the estate and the transferability of pension or retirement plans upon death. Unlike traditional couples, same-sex couples have not been afforded the protections and benefits granted to married couples by federal law until recently.[24] Therefore, the best course of action is to strongly encourage these couples to have well-thought-out and thorough estate plans. It is then up to the couple to openly communicate any shifts in the family structure and to the advisor to keep the partners abreast of any legal changes that may impact them financially.

IN HER OWN WORDS

I don't think that there is anything particularly unique about my relationship compared to most of my heterosexual friends. Every couple is unique, and it's always best to not make assumptions.
—*AMY, 39-YEAR-OLD MARRIED MOTHER OF ONE*

As a financial advisor, you will see family structures that show a greater diversity; therefore, it is important not to make assumptions about the couple based solely on their sexual orientation. According to Slater, "Typically what has been created as the alternative [to the traditional heterosexual couple] reflects great retention of individuality within the couple relationship, including some degree of financial separateness. You are more likely to see gay couples have separate money and joint money, rather than all joined."[25] Several advisors I interviewed stated that they treated same-sex couples the same as heterosexual couples. Although this may be well intended, it is a mistake. Same-sex couples have a different history from heterosexual couples and experience acceptance in society at varying levels. Therefore, it is better to risk feeling uncomfortable by asking all the questions you need to know in order to assess the couple's financial and personal goals and objectives. As Slater explains, "It is not being politically incorrect to start from scratch and ask particularly about how they've constructed the balance of being individual and being a joint entity."[26]

In modern society, it is human nature to want to be publicly viewed as open and accepting of gay lifestyles. However, for many of us who are straight, it can be uncomfortable to know exactly how to talk about these issues and how our behavior is being perceived by same-sex partners. Often we are taught to treat everyone the same, but similarly to how this does not work with male and female clients because it does not account for key gender differences, it is not effective with gay clients. If you find yourself declining a client because you don't know much about the legalities of same-sex marriage, this may be a way of avoiding dealing with this discomfort. Or maybe you do take same-sex partners on as clients but treat them as two separate people as opposed to a couple. This also may be a reflection of your anxiety in working with same-sex couples. The most important thing is to notice this tendency and not deny it. As human beings, we all have biases based on our upbringing, our life experience, and our beliefs. The goal of an astute financial advisor is to identify these thoughts and beliefs and then work to gain more knowledge and skills to help you overcome these deficits.

IN HIS OWN WORDS

I believe that if any of those service professionals have an "issue" with a same-sex couple, then the couple seeking services should run like hell! Most individuals I have met are savvy in this area. We have a large community of retired gays and lesbians in the Fort Lauderdale area with professionals (gay and straight) here ready to serve the community.

—JOHN, 69-YEAR-OLD RETIRED GRAPHIC DESIGNER

As a couple-friendly financial advisor, you need to understand the laws relative to gay marriage, civil unions, and domestic partnerships in your state. You also need to appreciate the historical backdrop that affects your work with these nontraditional couples and recognize any biases you may have regarding gay lifestyles. The bottom line is that this work is complex but highly rewarding. For those advisors who specialize in advising gay couples, it not only fits with their beliefs about all humans having rights to certain benefits and privileges, but makes good business sense. Once you are identified by a same-sex couple as a safe and knowledgeable financial services professional, you will receive referrals from their friends, family, and community.

Blended Families

Remember Mike and Carol Brady from the popular television show *The Brady Bunch* in the 1970s. Both had been married previously and brought three boys and three girls, respectively, of their own. At the time, the Brady clan was seen as a radical departure from the typical family, but today this type of family is often the norm. According to a Pew Research Center study in 2011, 42 percent of adults have a step-relationship, defined as either a stepparent, a step or half sibling, or a stepchild. This translates to 9.5 million adults.[27] Technically defined as couples with children from previous marriages living under one roof as a family, these blended partners may be legally married or living together. As you can imagine, hiring a couple-friendly advisor to help them merge their families is prudent.

IN HER OWN WORDS

When you are working with people from blended families, there tends to be more emotional issues at the core. Individuals want to protect their children, their money, and if there is not a friendly dynamic in place, you can feel the tension.

—*KELLY SHIKANY, CFP, VOGELSANG ASSET MANAGEMENT*

Blended families face a myriad of decisions similar to those faced by same-sex couples when it comes to managing the family's finances. Although it is prudent to have a prenuptial or postnuptial agreement as well as a well-thought-out estate plan that spells out how the family finances and assets will be handled during the marriage and in the event it dissolves, many couples don't take this step. This is unfortunate, as it often leads to misunderstanding and conflict in the family resulting from the lack of clear communication. Therefore, it is important to coach these couples to formalize their financial and estate plans as not only a legal tool, but also a way for the family to discuss and understand what is yours, mine, and ours, and, most important, why. While you may be reluctant to engage in this type of emotional dialogue with your clients, it truly is a gift to the couple you advise. By having these conversations, the partners are no longer left to wonder why certain financial decisions are made and the intent behind them. They know.

IN HER OWN WORDS

I recently was talking to two female twins in their sixties. When I admired the necklace one of them was wearing, she said smiling, "Oh yeah, my step-grandmother gave this to me." Her twin looked at me and said angrily, "It was our (biological) grandmother's necklace and our step-grandmother had no right to give it away. She basically stole it from our grandmother." What struck me was these two were born at the exact same time and they had two completely different experiences with the step-grandmother and how she treated the two of them, and the family possessions.

—EMILY BOUCHARD, COAUTHOR, ESTATE PLANNING FOR THE BLENDED FAMILY

Interestingly enough, the 2011 study by the Pew Research Center found that biology can make a difference when it comes to financial obligations. "Among adults who have both a grown biological child and a grown stepchild, the biological child exerts a stronger pull. Nearly eight in ten (78 percent) of these parents say they would feel obligated to provide assistance to a grown child. Closer to six in ten (62 percent) say they would feel equally obligated to their grown stepchild."[28] As you can imagine, two partners with varying degrees of obligation to the next generation may find it tricky to come to an agreement about money and financial planning.

The best course for you, as their advisor, to take is one of neutrality. As Emily Bouchard, coauthor of *Estate Planning for Blended Families*, stresses, "You need to be able to honor the conflict of interest and the position of all the perspectives as valid and true and real." This is opposed to the stance some advisors take, which is working with their existing client and trying to protect him or her from the new partner. As Bouchard states, "This stance creates real discord within a blended family situation."[29]

The key question for these partners is who is financially responsible for what now and how that might change in the future. On the surface, this question seems fairly straightforward; however, the answer is often complicated. Financial commitments, including alimony, spousal support, and childcare, are an important part of the conversation as well as how the couple intends on handling financial obligations in the blended family. The couple's complex family tree calls for more in-depth discussions regarding how to be equitable and fair in relationships that by nature are often uneven and sometimes contentious. Financial decisions and estate planning decisions are often emotionally laden, and couples in this situation need an advisor who can see the forest for the trees.

Stephanie Sharp, senior regional consultant for a large corporation, offered this advice to advisors based on her recent personal experience blending two homes. "Don't underestimate the little things and do what works for you financially." In May 2012, Stephanie married Shawn, her second husband, and now lives with him and their five children, who range in age from 10 to 13. While she felt prepared for merging their families from a child-centric point of view, Stephanie was surprised how she and her husband had overlooked some of the little but important things. Questions they had not anticipated ranged from how and when to do the laundry each week to what type of checks to order for the joint bank account. "Flash-forward to today and things are much easier. We have learned to let go of something if either of us feels very strongly about handling a specific responsibility; he has learned to accept that I will sort laundry into four types of loads rather than seven or eight and that I don't like for the laundry to pile up. I have learned that he can slice and dice our joint spending 6,000 different ways using Quicken, down to the penny, and that makes him very, very happy."[30]

Stephanie recommends that advisors coach blended families about money personalities and how to find the unique balance that works financially for each couple and their blended family. "While I'd like to say that I had romantic notions of my husband and me melding everything about our respective financial pictures together, the pragmatic mother in me wouldn't let me do that." She goes on to explain how different her and her husband's money personalities are and how each spouse in their previous marriages took charge when it came to family finances. The compromise was to share household expenses but keep virtually everything else separate. As Stephanie says, "I have had to grapple with the choice between being a party pooper (not doing the sport court, for now) versus being pushed into an area of extreme financial discomfort (going ahead and building the sport court now). In turn, he has had to balance between instant gratification (getting the sport court now) versus delaying it until the funds have been saved." The secret to their success, as far as I can tell, is a deep commitment to each other and their children, insight into their money personalities, and a healthy dose of compromise.

While Stephanie's situation is unique to her and her husband, it does provide insight into how many questions need to be answered when two families merge. As a trusted advisor, you have the advantage of an outsider's perspective. This allows you to help these couples engage in curious exploration of how money was managed in previous relationships and how the couple wants to operate similarly to or different from in the past. These questions help with both the logistical and the tactical issues, and also the emotional ones that arise when two separate homes become one. Here are 10 questions to get the dialogue started:

1. What is your number one concern as a blended family financially?
2. What is your number one concern as a blended family emotionally?
3. How many children do you have, and which ones are from previous relationships?
4. How many children do you have from your current relationship, and how would you describe their relationship with their step-siblings?
5. What are the terms of your divorce settlement relative to childcare, alimony, and spousal support?
6. How would you describe your relationship with your ex-spouse(s)?
7. How do you think your relationship with your ex-spouse(s) might impact your financial planning and estate planning process?
8. What ideally would you like to see happen in your family now and in the future?
9. What mistakes have you made in your previous relationships or marriages that you would like to avoid in this union?
10. How can I be a resource for you and your blended family?

As a couple-friendly advisor, it is vital that you appreciate the complexities inherent in these partnerships. The primary goal is to assist these couples in communicating the feelings behind their financial decision-making process and then to craft a financial plan and strategy that meet their individual needs as well as those of their blended family.

Summary

Historically, male partners were the breadwinners and wealth creators and, therefore, called the financial shots for the family. Over the past several decades, this has become no longer true and is a dangerous assumption for a couple-friendly advisor to make. Instead, you need to discover the rules of engagement used by the couple in front of you and creatively work with them to develop financial strategies and solutions that meet their unique life circumstances. Being open to nontraditional lifestyles and leaving your preconceived notions of what constitutes a family at the door are vital if you are to be successful advising modern couples now and into the future.

Your Next Step: A Closer Look at Modern Couples

Now that you know more about the intricacies of modern couples, it is time to consider what additional questions you may want to ask the nontraditional couples in your practice. To complete this exercise, pick three couple clients to review. Select couples whom you enjoy working with, who have a substantial amount of assets with your firm, and whom you want to strengthen your advisory relationship with. Now use the following chart to examine what you know about these clients and what you still need to learn to become or remain their trusted advisor.

	Couple 1		Couple 2		Couple 3	
	Partner A	Partner B	Partner A	Partner B	Partner A	Partner B
Age:						
Occupation:						
Marital status:						
Sexual orientation:						
If gay: ◆ How "out" are they to family of origin? ◆ How do family members view gay lifestyle? ◆ How might family's feelings about their sexual orientation impact children?						
Annual income:						
Previously married?						
Financial obligations from previous marriage:						
Children (include names/ages): ◆ Biological: ◆ Step: ◆ Adopted: ◆ Foster:						
Financial decision-making philosophy:						
Estate planning and legal documents: ◆ Wills: ◆ Trusts: ◆ Powers of attorney: ◆ Prenuptial/Postnuptial agreements: ◆ Domestic partnership agreements: ◆ Healthcare proxies: ◆ Other:						
Joint assets:						
Individually held assets:						
Major financial concerns:						
Major family concerns:						
Goals for financial planning:						

After you complete your review, notice any gaps in your knowledge and make a plan to address these areas in your next interaction with the couple. If you found this exercise helpful, use this chart with all your couple clients as a way to make sure you are capturing the uniqueness of each partnership and the implications of their family structure on the planning process.

$$\left(5 \right)$$

Couples Across the Life Span

A successful marriage requires falling in love many times, always with the same person.

—Mignon McLaughlin, American journalist and author

HAVE YOU EVER FALLEN IN LOVE? IT'S GRAND. THE OBJECT OF YOUR affection is perfect. You are on cloud nine, and life is filled with joy, laughter, and fun. You think this feeling is never going to end. And then you move in together. Whether you tie the knot or simply move your stuff into your romantic partner's apartment, something shifts when you live with this person 24 hours a day, 7 days a week. It is not bad, just different. What you admired—his spontaneity, her dependability, his love for YouTube cat videos, or her constant need to be on the telephone—becomes challenging. You still love this person, but you are now realizing that he or she is perfectly flawed. If you are brave-hearted, you forge on and learn to accept the good with the bad. Soon enough you are celebrating your twenty-fifth wedding anniversary and falling in love all over again.

Couplehood is fascinating, frustrating, and not for the faint-hearted. Throw money into the mix and it can be a wild ride. As a financial advisor working with couples, it is important to appreciate the life cycles of couplehood and how you can help your clients during each phase of their lives together. Your job is to assist couple clients in managing money and planning for their financial future. Therefore, understanding how couples operate based on where they are in the circle of life and partnership is important. You can choose to delve into these areas with your clients if your advising style is more in-depth or simply use this knowledge to inform your work. Either way, couples change and grow over the years. Their financial planning and investment needs differ, and you need to know where in the couple life cycle they are in order to counsel them successfully.

The Wild World of Couplehood

One day I was driving in the car with my husband on the way to a family event. I said, "This couple thing is weird." He looked at me with a quizzical expression and said, "Why?" I responded, "Think about it. You meet, become a couple, and are excited to go to family events and show each other off. Eventually, you find out your in-laws are as mixed up as your own family, only in different ways. You then go to family events strategizing as a team on how you can watch each other's back and cope with the specific craziness of the family you are visiting. On the drive home, you debrief your individual and collective experiences. The insane part is it is only a matter of time before you suit up as a couple and make the same journey again." My husband just looked at me and laughed.

My point was that couplehood is a strange, wonderful, and wild ride. Universally, we all want to have a special someone in our lives, yet when we do, this relationship challenges us like no other. Sometimes it is predictable. Other times it has unexpected twists and turns. And money plays a big role in the journey. From the time two people start dating until they ultimately say goodbye to each other through death or divorce, finances are a part of the relationship. Couples consciously or unconsciously decide how to spend and enjoy money, how to save and amass wealth, and how to use money to exert power and control in the relationship. Some partners fight about money; others worry about it. Some couples join forces and create a strong financial and emotional bond; others never seem to trust each other financially. Whatever the dynamic, these couples show up in your offices looking for financial guidance and expect you to have all the answers. The real challenge is to share your expertise, while at the same time appreciating the complexities of couples and their journey together.

Couple Development

Over their life span, couples face a variety of financial conflicts that are reflective of their psychological developmental stage. These differences often represent a couple working through a developmental task aimed at increasing intimacy and solidifying their couple identity. These tasks include the following:[1]

◆ Finding and maintaining personal boundaries
◆ Developing a couple identity separate from their families of origin
◆ Accepting and respecting each individual's needs while also encouraging increased intimacy as a couple
◆ Respecting and negotiating differences
◆ Developing communication and problem-solving skills
◆ Learning how to calm each other
◆ Understanding how power and control are expressed and balanced in the relationship

Here is an example of how a couple may disagree about a financial decision and be working through a developmental milestone. A couple comes to your office for their annual review and asks questions about how best to save for their dream home. The wife talks about how her parents want to give money toward the down payment, and the husband becomes visibly annoyed. Later in the meeting, the wife again raises the question of accepting money from her parents, stating, "It will make them happy to see me in the new house. So what is the big deal?" The husband rolls his eyes and turns to you and asks a question about their saving options. You notice that each time the wife brings up her parents' desire to contribute, the husband squirms in his chair. You think back to previous meetings and realize this same dynamic occurred.

On the surface, this couple is disagreeing about money, but if you look beyond the words, there is a developmental issue underneath. You realize that the conflict is not just about the house, but about the couple's different views on how involved parents should be in the financial lives of their adult children. This relates to developmental tasks such as setting boundaries, forming a solid couple identity, and differentiating from the families of origin. Now you can ask questions that are more likely to move the couple forward toward a decision. Instead of asking about how much the couple can save each month or how much the parents are willing to contribute, you inquire about how each individual views parental involvement in the couple's financial life. This question is much more effective and opens up the dialogue to include the more pertinent developmental issues that need to be dealt with to avoid this same argument coming up again and again at advisory meetings.

In addition to working through developmental tasks, couples also pass through a variety of emotional stages relative to how they view their partner and each other. A couple falls in love and then needs to work through the reality of what it means to share a life with someone. For those who make it for the long haul, individual differences cause conflict but are resolved over time as acceptance and intimacy increase. Let's look at how this plays out in relationships and how money is used to work through this less tangible psychological process.

Stage 1: Honeymoon

The honeymoon stage is when being in a relationship is easy. You are filled with warm feelings and focused solely on getting to know your partner. You bond through shared experiences, sexual intimacy, and being introduced to each other's family and friends. Falling in love is often described as floating on air. The truth is, you are experiencing a dopamine rush in your brain, and you indeed are on a high. Dopamine is associated with pleasure, and scientists say it plays a role in gambling, drug use, and falling in love. Also at play is oxytocin, which has a calming effect and promotes intimacy between partners, and testosterone, which pushes the sex drive of both partners up a notch.[2] This stage of love is intense and can't be sustained over the lifetime of a relationship.

During the honeymoon stage, money and finance usually are not part of the conversation. Couples default to automatic thoughts and behaviors about who should pay for what on a date. More traditionally oriented couples silently agree that the man picks up the check. More nontraditional couples base this decision on who makes more money or who asked whom out, but the money discussion seldom goes into much more depth. There are so many things you want to talk with your new love about, and money is usually not one of them.

One exception to this rule is in couples where one or both people have been married previously. This type of couple often realizes the importance of talking about money up front. In addition, these individuals often have complex financial situations such as alimony, palimony, and childcare that trigger these discussions. These couples tend to be older and often are already working with a financial advisor. This puts the advisor in a better position to ask questions to facilitate an open dialogue about money in the relationship. For a list of good questions, refer to "Your Next Step" at the end of this chapter.

IN HER OWN WORDS

We both had been burned by problems with money in past marriages, so we talked about finances during our dating years.
—KATHY, 56-YEAR-OLD REMARRIED BUSINESS OWNER WITH TWO STEPCHILDREN

Young love developmentally is at its infancy. Couples often fail to realize how this partnership, if it endures, will require them to examine their own money beliefs and to compromise so that they can move from "me" to "we." If you have an opportunity to work with a couple during the honeymoon stage, you can plant some seeds on what types of financial differences they may encounter and lay a solid foundation for open and honest communication about money. But don't worry if you find it hard to get couples to commit to this type of work with you until the dopamine rush wears off.

Stage 2: Struggle

When two people make a commitment to each other, they are forced to deal with money in their couplehood. Events such as moving in together or tying the knot mean that these two individuals now have to figure out how to combine their financial lives. Questions such as who pays what bills and from what account become necessary to answer. These financial inquiries mirror the couple's entering a new developmental stage of negotiating autonomy versus togetherness. The overarching question is, "How do we emotionally and financially fit together?"

Couples use their respective parents as role models when it comes to handling finances as a couple. If the partners grew up in traditional heterosexual homes, then they may default to traditional gender role models when it comes to making and managing money. They also may decide to reject this paradigm and create their own system. In same-sex couples, the decisions to share or not share financial responsibilities are made without the benefit of preexisting gender role expectations. Therefore, these nontraditional couples are left to be creative and often think outside the box when it comes to making and managing money as a couple. This can be challenging for these couples, as it can be easier to accept or reject a method than to design a new one from scratch.

As the personal lives of couples become more intertwined, they make more financial decisions together, and inevitably differences of opinion arise. Couples begin to struggle to find out who they are individually and as a couple. This conflict is healthy and helps each partner move from fantasy to reality.[3] During this stage, partners spend time trying to convince the other person that their way of doing things is the right way. Couples often have varied perspectives on how to stack the dishwasher, how to do the laundry, and, of course, how to spend and save money. Healthy partners eventually accept each other's viewpoints and, in many instances, learn to compromise. Other couples remain stuck in the struggle.

IN HIS OWN WORDS

I believe in asking for forgiveness, not permission. In other words, I'm going to buy something if I want it and then apologize afterwards.

—TOM, 64-YEAR-OLD MARRIED FATHER OF TWO, GRANDFATHER OF FIVE, RETIRED

Shell Tain, founder of Sensible Coaching, shared a story of a woman who wanted money coaching who was firmly entrenched in this stage. "This woman came up to me at an event and said, 'Can you help me and my husband? He's just doing it wrong. He keeps doing all these spreadsheets and they're just ridiculous and he's just wrong.'" As any insightful coach would do, Tain explained how the husband's way was not wrong but different from the wife's way. With coaching, this woman learned how to grieve the loss of how she wanted her husband to act around money and accept his behavior as right for him.[4]

Couples work through money differences over a period of time as their couple identity strengthens. This work can happen over the course of a few years, a few decades, or not at all. The key is to help couples identify money differences and talk about the emotions related to letting go of their individual financial identities and accepting both the good and the bad of what it means to be in this financial partnership together. Once partners grieve the loss of the honeymoon stage by working through the struggle, they find a more powerful financial alliance and often an increase in trust and intimacy.

It is important to know that some couples never make concessions and remain in conflict. In this type of relationship, time marches forward, but developmentally, the couple stays stuck. These are the clients who come into your office year after year and have the same financial fight each time. These couples often are good candidates for a referral to a marriage counselor or family wealth consultant, as the money struggle is a reflection of a deeper marital problem. Refer to Chapter 12, "Special Issues in Advising Couples," for guidelines on how to make a good referral. Those who refuse a referral or do attend couple counseling but fail to benefit often have unconsciously made a pact to not grow and change emotionally or financially. As long as both partners remain at peace with this silent agreement, the union works. It is when one partner decides he or she wants more that these couples separate or divorce.

As a financial advisor, you can coach couples on how to communicate about their financial lives and work toward mutual acceptance. Talking about money openly and accepting financial differences is often not passed down from the previous generation. In later chapters, you will learn techniques for uncovering money beliefs and managing, facilitating, and resolving conflicts. These are vital skills for a couple-friendly advisor, as they help clients move to the next stage of couplehood more quickly. The by-product of this type of work is that it increases the financial and emotional health of the couple and strengthens their view of you as the trusted advisor.

Stage 3: Acceptance

As couples identify and resolve different money beliefs, values, and attitudes, they enter a stage called *acceptance*. The partners decide when they want to default to one individual's way of doing things versus when to develop a new couple mode of operation. This couple identity respects the needs of each individual but also is a blend of the strengths of both partners. This process can be bumpy and last a long time, but eventually the couple moves into a place of mature love. Mature love is when you appreciate and celebrate each other's strengths, flaws, and quirkiness.

Let's admit it: some things are harder to accept than others. Dirty dishes in the sink are one thing, but how your partner spends, saves, and invests money is another. This is where you come in. As a couple-friendly advisor, you can create a safe environment in your office to discuss financial differences. Part of this work is helping couples identify, understand, and talk about their unique money histories. The more difficult step is for couples to deal with the feelings associated with not getting their way financially. With time and your guidance, however, they can learn to let go of the struggle and create a couple financial identity together.

IN HIS OWN WORDS

I think our involvement with a financial planner early in our marriage kept us from getting into many of the financial traps other couples do. We are somewhat secure because of it and have had no real dust-ups over money issues.

—*JEFF, 43-YEAR-OLD MARRIED MANAGEMENT CONSULTANT AND FATHER OF TWO*

In addition to solidifying their couple identity, many couples start families during this stage. This brings on a host of new dilemmas and financial decisions for the couple. There is nothing like rearing children together to bring the need to respect and negotiate differences into focus. It is no longer just about the two of them but about the future of the children. Even if couples decide not to have children, they still need to learn how to express and balance power and control in the relationship. Often, how the couple makes, manages, and spends money is fertile ground for this type of work.

Understanding how couples evolve over time allows you to gear your questions and expectations to fit with the developmental tasks and emotional stage the clients are in. Money is a tool that couples use to survive, but it is also a mirror for the dynamics of the couple and where they are in their emotional development. By assessing where your clients are in their couple development and acceptance of each other's differences, you can more effectively counsel and advise couples.

Times, They Are Changing

Couples go through a series of transitions based on their life circumstances and personal choices. Common transitions include marriage or cohabitation, starting a family, launching children into the world, caring for elderly parents, and retirement. Each phase is marked by unique financial and emotional challenges.

Committed Love

In the past, a couple stood in front of their family and friends on their wedding day and declared their love publicly by legally getting married. It was the socially accepted way to enter the phase of committed love. However, modern couples have other options these days, including living together and raising a family while remaining legally separate entities. In fact, marriage is on the decline in the United States, according to the 2012 report from The State of Our Unions. The total number of marriages fell from 2.45 million in 1990 to 2.11 million in 2010. The decline is caused by couples delaying first marriages, the increase in cohabitation, and the slight decrease in divorced individuals remarrying.[5]

As the definition of committed love shifts, the couples you see in your advisory office may look different from those in the past. As you learned in Chapter 4, "The Modern Couple," you need to remain open to varying definitions of what it means to be a couple. This makes your job as a financial advisor more interesting and challenging, as the legalities and financial nuances are unique to each couple.

At the committed love stage of couplehood, clients come to see advisors to help them figure out how to financially plan for the future. Emotionally, this is a phase of increased intimacy for the couple, with money often being the next frontier in their journey. In fact, how couples combine their finances can mirror the level of trust and intimacy in their relationship in general. For example, if two partners maintain joint funds, it may indicate that they value financial equality. The value of equality may also permeate other areas of the relationship, such as shared domestic chores and childcare. If they opt for a hybrid system, meaning that they pool some of their money and leave some of it in individual accounts, it may reflect their desire for a balance between intimacy and togetherness and independence. Finally, couples who maintain separate financial lives may lack trust in their partners. In all these situations, you need to tread lightly. Further exploration of the motives of each partner in their financial structures is warranted, as the reasons behind these decisions are more telling than the division of the actual accounts.

With joint accounts, one partner is responsible for maintaining the couple's checking and savings accounts and may even be the financial advisor's main contact. While this can be a source of conflict for a couple and a way in which power and control issues are expressed, it also can be a necessary way to divide family tasks. In the article "Financial Management Practices of Couples with Great Marriages," the financial habits of 64 couples located throughout the United States were studied. Participants self-identified as couples with a great marriage. The authors concluded, "It did not make much difference which spouse handled the money. . . . It was more important to the couple that one person had the time, the expertise, and the desire."[6] While this sample is small, it speaks to the fact that if both members of the couple are in agreement as to who manages the money and how the money is handled, then a more traditional joint arrangement makes sense.

Other couples decide on a hybrid approach, meaning that they maintain both joint and separate accounts. This may be a result of more couples living together and being financially responsible for shared expenses prior to marriage or to the value many modern couples place on autonomy and privacy. Notice that I said privacy, not secrecy. Privacy means that each member of the couple is allowed to manage some money independently, without reporting this activity to his or her partner. This arrangement is common in dual-income households and is seen by many as a great way to balance the need for intimacy and togetherness with the need for individual boundaries and independence. This arrangement decreases the dependency of one partner on the other and empowers both to be financially responsible.

Some couples decide not to merge their financial lives at all. This is often seen with blended families, in same-sex partnerships, and when family wealth is a factor. These situations result in complex financial pictures where in many cases, combining assets is not desirable or legally prudent.

What a couple agrees to when they enter the committed love stage may change and shift over time. Therefore, it is important to find out how each partner views the couple's current financial arrangements. Ask questions such as, "How did you decide to manage money this way?," "How does this arrangement currently feel to you now that you have been practicing it for a while?," and "What story have you made up about your partner's role in the finances?" These inquiries tap into unspoken thoughts that one or both partners might have about their finances. Because committed partners are notorious for making faulty assumptions about their mates, the data needs to be collected. By uncovering this information, you are helping your clients verbalize their concerns and clearly communicate what feels most comfortable to them and why. Because talking about money is often a new skill for committed couples, it is a place where you can provide tons of value.

IN HER OWN WORDS

I have a client who is upper middle class in a traditional marriage. She gets an allowance of $250 a week from her husband, who is a businessman, and knows very little about money. When she met her husband, she felt secure for the first time in her life, so she was willing to go along with whatever he wanted financially. Now that she is feeling more powerful, she wants more control but is petrified to tell him.
—*DIANA MANSFIELD, LMHC, STILL WATERS COUNSELING AND WELLNESS*

The ultimate goal at this stage is to help couples design a system that works for their unique life situation and personalities. Make sure you let them know that the system should be reevaluated annually as circumstances change. If you are successful in empowering couples at this stage, future life transitions are likely to go more smoothly.

Family First

Soon after many couples commit to each other, they welcome children into their family. This event leads many of them to seriously examine their financial lives for the first time. Questions such as how will we pay for private school and college tuition, buy a new family-size home, and save for our retirement populate parents' minds. The good news is, you are equipped with many concrete financial solutions to assist them. But what differentiates you from the advisor next door is your ability to recognize, appreciate, and, if necessary, work with the more complex emotional and relational issues commonly found at this stage of marriage. These include changes in the power dynamic in the relationship because of parenthood, fear of financial dependency if one spouse decides to stay at home with the children, and raising financially thoughtful children.

In His Own Words

We used to do it (balance the checkbook and pay bills) together, but when we had kids, there wasn't as much time to sit down together.

—MATT, 40-YEAR-OLD SOCIAL WORKER AND MARRIED FATHER OF TWO

Parenthood is a subject for a book unto itself. Let's just say that this is a common experience for committed couples and one that challenges the individuals and the partnership on many levels. A couple's relationship satisfaction is said to be at its lowest during the teen-child-rearing years, when parents are faced with not only financially supporting their children but also teaching them how to be financially literate adults.[7] This is a recipe for stress and conflict and a place where your services can help relieve the pressure. Having a trusted advisor create a safe space for the couple to discuss life goals and financial matters is often seen as the calm in the storm of family life. You can help them realistically assess what they need to do today to save for their dreams of tomorrow. Also, you can provide them tools for effectively talking about money, negotiating differences, and coaching the next generation on making and managing money responsibly.

Over the years, I have interviewed a number of women who talk about the shift in economic power in the marriage once the children are born. Often these women had high-powered careers prior to starting a family and opted to stay at home with the kids based on their personal values. What they did not anticipate was how not earning money and being reliant on their husbands to provide for them financially would feel. These women who were empowered at work started to feel as if they needed permission to buy anything. One woman shared with me her debate over buying a toilet brush at Home Depot: "In the past, I would have just bought it without a thought. But now that my income is zero, it took me 10 minutes to decide if I should spend the money and, if so, whether to get the cheapest one or to purchase the one I wanted. All over a toilet brush!" It is almost as if these high-powered career women turn the clock back to the turn of the century and become disempowered financially.

Diana Mansfield, an experienced couples counselor, puts it this way, "What surprises me the most is there is a patriarchal system where the husband is primary and the wife is secondary. The husband doesn't necessarily need to ask permission to spend, but the wife seems to feel she needs to."[8] Although this dynamic may not occur in all couples, it is one to notice. If unexpressed, the feelings of resentment caused by the shift in financial power in the couple can contribute to compulsive spending, lying about money, and overall marital discord.

Do men who stay at home with the children have the same tendency to defer to their breadwinning wives? Not necessarily, says Joan D. Atwood in her article "Couples and Money: The Last Taboo": ". . . when the wife is the primary breadwinner, she is more likely to relinquish her power or choose to share responsibility of the financial management than if the husband is the primary breadwinner."[9] The same is true for housework. When men are the primary earners, women do most of the household labor; however, when women are the primary breadwinners, men do an equal share of the housework.[10] It seems there is a gender difference when it comes to how men and women view the division of labor in the family. Atwood's theory is that this difference may be due to the internal conflict many women feel relative to holding and maintaining power in relationships. I wonder if it is attributed more to brain chemistry. Maybe the female brain, which is wired for connection, pushes women to take a more collaborative approach to household tasks, whereas the male brain, which is wired for individualization, skews differently. As women's economic power continues to rise, this may become clearer.

In addition to finding a new rhythm as parents, couples are faced with how to raise financially literate and thoughtful children. In this complex world, this is one of a multitude of tasks that couples worry about. The dilemma is that this subject often falls to the bottom of the list, as drugs, sex, and rock-and-roll seem scarier and more pressing. In your role as the couple's advisor, you can plant seeds on how parents can teach their children about money and finance. Because this area is in demand, there is an entire chapter dedicated to it later in the book. For now, it is sufficient to say that teaching couples how to talk to their children about money strengthens your bond with the couple and provides opportunities for you to meet the next generation. Your financial expertise helps parents feel more equipped to tackle difficult questions such as when and how to give money to their children, how to answer questions about family wealth, and how to negotiate financial support as the children reach adulthood.

Graduation Day

The goal of any parent is to raise a healthy, happy child and launch this young person into the world as a productive adult. This process takes a minimum of 18 years and sometimes up to 30! In previous generations, children graduated from high school, went to college, and four years later landed a "real job." The onus was on the young graduate to find a job, fund an apartment, and pay for the amenities of life. However, over the past decade, more adult children are returning to live with their parents after graduation and effectively delaying the transition into adulthood.

According to a Pew Research Center study, 7 in 10 adult children who live with their parents are younger than 30 years of age. Fifty percent of these grown children work full or part time, 25 percent are unemployed, and the remainder are full-time students.[11] Because these young adults may go out on their own for a while, then return, they have been labeled the *boomerang generation*. Some members of the boomerang generation, approximately 48 percent, pay rent to their parents, and 89 percent say they contribute financially to cover household expenses.[12] This still leaves over half living rent free and relying on mom and dad financially.

Some people blame the bad economy for the increase in children moving back home. During the 2008 to 2010 recession, unemployment rates for 20- to 24-year-olds were at an all-time high, with November 2009 being the high point at 17.2 percent. Furthermore, the percentage of young adults in their twenties who were working was at an historic low.[13] Although these economic factors are real, there is also some truth to the fact that moving back home is a generational trend that may continue post-recession. According to Joline Godfrey and David Wegbreit, "The expectations of today's twenty-somethings are grounded in lifelong experience of being told they could do anything, be anything, and have anything. They are phenomenally well educated. They were raised to follow instructions and follow them well. . . . The environment they've been launched into offers chaos and a scarcity they have not been prepared for."[14] The one thing that is familiar is home.

In addition to being comfortable living with mom and dad, this arrangement is largely accepted by their peers. In previous decades, moving back home was seen as a failure, but nowadays, it is viewed as a wise financial move. You get to live with all the creature comforts of home and pay little, if anything, for them. It can be debated if this boomerang mindset is healthy or not. Only time will tell. In the meantime, it can be costly for your clients.

Your clients may need to be coached on how to set financial boundaries with their adult children. Some parents see their financial support as love and believe that if they withhold it, they are being bad parents. They may have experienced these feelings growing up when their parents didn't give them money and want to spare their children from feeling emotionally abandoned like they did. Or your clients may still be financially dependent on their parents and view supporting adult children as their duty. Whatever the reason, it is often healthy for parents to set some financial limits on their adult children, as this teaches them important skills that contribute to being financially self-sufficient.

Several advisors have shared with me their frustration with clients who continue to financially fund their grown children's lifestyles. They see this behavior as detrimental to the next generation's learning basic money management skills such as saving, budgeting, and spending responsibly. They plead for moms and dads to stop giving so much money to their children and show the parents reports demonstrating how this behavior is depleting their own retirement funds. While this tactic is well intended, it often misses the mark, as it overlooks the emotional part of the equation. Your clients need help understanding and gaining insight into what makes it so hard to set financial limits with their children before they can curtail or slow down this behavior. Questions aimed at the underlying motivations are much more effective than showing them scary charts and graphs. Consider these questions instead:

- Did your parents financially provide for you as a young adult beyond your college or early working years? If so, what was this like for you as their child?
- If you could set a limit with your adult child, what would you have to tolerate emotionally?

◆ If your financial gifts could talk to your adult child, what would they say?

◆ Is there another way of communicating this to your adult child other than financially?

◆ What is your greatest fear in not continuing to fund your adult child's lifestyle?

These inquiries cut to the root of the behavior and are aimed at understanding the parents' underlying motives. By helping your couple clients examine their mindset around financing their adult children's expenses, you are opening a new window into their financial habits that may assist them in setting better boundaries going forward. For some parents, this type of insight is enough for them to act differently with their adult children. For others, it may be that they will always provide financial assistance beyond what you see as reasonable. Remember not to judge your clients because ultimately, how they spend their money is up to them.

When adult children do leave the nest, many parents experience a sense of loss as their roles as parents are shifting and they are less needed by their offspring. It is natural to experience sadness and some mixed feelings about this next stage of couple life. Days and nights that were previously filled with parental responsibilities are now free to spend in self-interested pursuits. Some parents find this adjustment fairly easy and are excited to see what lies ahead. Others go through a period of mourning, and need time to reevaluate their priorities and reassess their life paths now that their work as parents is primarily done. As a couple-friendly advisor, you can normalize this transition and offer couples an opportunity to talk about what it feels like to launch their children into the world. This is a great time to reevaluate life goals and adjust financial and investment strategies for this newly defined future. It is also a time when many couples rekindle romantic love, as they have more time and energy to put into the relationship.

Sandwiched In

Another societal phenomenon that is trending upward is the number of couples taking care of one or more elderly parents while at the same time raising kids. Known as the *sandwich generation*, clients balancing these two roles find themselves both emotionally and financially taxed. The members of the sandwich generation are mostly middle-aged, with 71 percent of this group being between 40 and 59 years of age.[15] Interestingly enough, more affluent adults with an annual income of $100,000 or more are impacted by this problem. Forty-three percent of this demographic reported living with a parent 65 years or older and a dependent child.[16] While both men and women act as caregivers, 66 percent are female, with women providing an average of 21.9 hours per week of care versus the 17.4 hours that men provide.[17] These women and men feel pulled between their work, children, and parents and often experience a high level of stress as a result.

IN HER OWN WORDS

Being in the sandwich generation is stress on steroids. You think you have launched your kids and you can enjoy your career and your partner, and then reality steps in. You have aging parents who need you, kids who can't find jobs or work so much they need help with their kids, and your job is now asking you to do more with less.

—*MEREDITH, 50-YEAR-OLD REMARRIED PROFESSIONAL AND STEPMOTHER OF TWO*

Complicated financial and emotional questions abound for those caring for both children and elderly parents. These include, but are not limited to, the following:

◆ Should we pay for professional caregiving services?
◆ Should one of us stay home as the primary caregiver?

◆ Can the aging parent still manage his or her own finances, and if not, who should take over this responsibility?

◆ Do we pay for private school for our children or put that money toward the parents' increasing healthcare costs?

◆ Do our parents have wills and estate plans that protect family assets and communicate preferences for treatment and end-of-life wishes? If not, how do we help them make these decisions?

These and other questions may lead to these clients feeling tired, overworked, and ambivalent. It is important that you initiate a conversation about eldercare with all your couple clients. Often couples don't want to bring up the subject and hope that by not talking about it, the stress will diminish. However, being proactive is always best in these delicate situations. This will help your clients figure out how to help their parents and also allow them to start the important process of planning for the distribution of their estate and communication of their wishes should they become dependent on their children in the future.

IN HIS OWN WORDS

The impact [of] being in the sandwich generation is you put the needs of your children and elderly parents before your own needs. You want to give your children every possible opportunity, and you feel a duty to care for elderly parents as they cared for you. I guess the result is losing some of your own identity along the way, particularly if any of your children have special needs.
—SCOTT, **48**-YEAR-OLD MARRIED PROFESSIONAL AND FATHER OF TWO

In Chapter 12, "Special Issues in Advising Couples," more insight is offered about proactively addressing this complicated client circumstance.

The Next Phase of Life

The common term for this next phase of life is *retirement*. However, according to many retirement experts, this term is antiquated. Mitch Anthony, author of several books including *The New Retirementality: Planning Your Life and Living Your Dreams . . . at Any Age You Want*, says, "retirement is a manmade transition." He believes the conversation with clients needs to change from how much money you need to retire to how you want to spend your time during this next phase of life. This shift allows clients to consider all the possibilities and does not conjure up images of an old man wasting his days away in a rocking chair.[18]

It is true that the population is living longer and is more active than in previous generations. I only need to look at my father, who is 82 and so active that at times it is hard for me to keep up. He skis, bikes, hikes, golfs, and is always in the middle of some building project. Dad is not alone, as he belongs to the 70+ Ski Club and I have joined him on some club trips. These "seniors" are far from old.

IN HER OWN WORDS

I think it's important to think less about what you're retiring from and more on what you're retiring to so that you begin to think about what's ahead.
—DORIAN MINTZER, PHD, COAUTHOR, THE COUPLE'S RETIREMENT PUZZLE

As couples make the transition to this next phase of life, they need your help envisioning the future. Some clients want to work, some want to play, and, more often than not, many opt for a little of both. Interestingly enough, the return to work is often not about needing the money, but more about feeling a sense of purpose in life. This trend is on the rise, as recent figures from T. Rowe Price indicate 69 percent of people go back to work at least part time in the first year of retirement not for financial reasons, but to stay challenged, healthy, and intellectually stimulated.[19]

This life transition allows couple to redefine their relationship and how they want to spend their time together—or, in some instances, apart. The divorce rate among those over 50 years of age has doubled since 1990, with many older baby boomers opting to go into retirement alone.[20] The children are grown up, and many couples find they no longer are in love. Others enjoy this next phase together and relish carving out a new life with more time to travel, play, and be with family. Either way, couples need to prepare for this next phase of life, and curious questioning can help. Here are 10 questions to consider:

1. How do you want to spend your time in this next phase of your life?
2. How does this vision fit with your partner's and how is it different?
3. What did retirement look like for your parents?
4. Do you want to mimic this lifestyle or do something different?
5. What brings you pleasure and gives you a sense of purpose in life?
6. How can you engage in these types of activities during this phase of life?
7. Do you want to work during this next phase of life? If so, part-time or full-time?
8. Have you discussed your vision for retirement with your children?
9. What is your greatest fear about retirement? Your partner's greatest fear?
10. How can I help you with these concerns?

As you know, it can be difficult to get clients to think about retirement when they are in the midst of other life transitions such as raising a family or caring for elderly parents. They want to put this dialogue off because they fear getting old, becoming sick, losing control, or facing their mortality. All of these factors are understandable, but according to Dorian Mintzer, coauthor of the book *The Couple's Retirement Puzzle: 10 Must-Have Conversations for Transition to the Second Half of Life*, it is important for financial advisors to strongly encourage couples to start these discussions early because it takes time to figure out each partner's individual goals and their shared goals for this stage of life.

A lack of structure often comes when the couple enters their senior years. Asking the couple to consider how much time they want to spend together versus apart each day is a basic but useful question. Financially, they need to be prepared, and emotionally, they will adjust better to this second act of life if they feel engaged with the world around them. Clients need to consider what brings them joy and fulfillment in addition to how they are going to fund these activities.[21] As with all life transitions, as a couple-friendly advisor, you assist couples with talking about their shared values and their differences, and helping them create a vision that allows both partners to feel fulfilled and gratified at this stage of life. Once this work is done, crafting a financial plan and investing strategy to support this vision follows.

The couples you advise will go through many life transitions and need your help navigating both the financial and the emotional landscape of these changes. Advisors who are equipped to offer guidance and support during the ups and downs of life are seen as valuable travel companions by couples, making them much more likely to invite you on this lifelong journey with them.

Tainted Love

At any point in a couple's development, they can decide to call it quits. There are many reasons for divorce, including different goals, values, and financial priorities. A couple may blame money as the reason for the breakup, but this is seldom the only cause. Usually it is a combination of factors that fester over time and become unbearable for one or both of the partners. Depending on the circumstances, the couple experiences a range of emotions from hurt to contempt to apathy. What is important is for you to show your care and concern for both members of the couple and maintain neutrality as they begin the long process of dividing up their assets.

Divorce not only is an emotionally trying time for the couple, but can be a difficult time for you as their advisor. You may have grown fond of the couple and been blindsided by the news of their split. Or the couple may attempt to put you in the middle as the situation heats up. Either way, you need to be aware of your ethical and fiduciary responsibilities to the couple and the individuals involved in the breakup.

Married couples have a fiduciary responsibility to each other, meaning that they have an obligation to be honest and forthright regarding all financial dealings affecting either partner. This means that if one partner asks you not to disclose information to the other, you may find yourself legally in hot water. This rule not only applies to those who are legally married but also can be applicable to same-sex couples and blended families. Therefore, it is important to know the rules in your jurisdiction.[22]

Violet P. Woodhouse, a certified family law specialist and financial planner in Newport Beach, California, recommends that advisors "consider having clients sign a letter that states that the spouses (or partners) have differing interests, including their ability to tolerate risk, the investments they might choose, and their level of investment sophistication and that they recognize these differences." She goes on to recommend that you have a partner who delegates responsibility for money management to the more financially astute partner sign a special power of attorney outlining this agreement. These steps are aimed at making sure you are not caught in the legal cross fire should the couple split.[23]

For this and other reasons, many advisors prefer to refer the partners to separate individual advisors to help them during this turbulent time. The door is left open for one or both of the partners to return, but after the divorce is finalized. The advisor explains that he or she is a consultant to the couple, and now that the couple is dissolving, it is best to refer them to separate impartial financial professionals. This approach is clean and helps you avoid sticky situations that often present themselves as part of a couple's divorce proceedings. When you are working in a large firm, it can be easier to orchestrate this referral than when you are in a small or solo practice. However, you need to make sure your decision to work with one or both partners during this time period is in the best interest of the couple.

As Tim Maurer, financial planner and coauthor of *The Ultimate Financial Plan: Balancing Your Money and Life*, will tell you, making these determinations is not always easy. He shared one recent experience, "I really had developed a personal affinity for this couple. When I learned they were splitting up and the wife wanted to come to *me* for advice, I came to realize I could not be effective. After learning of the news, I had one meeting with her and concluded I could not separate my desire to see them whole and healthy from giving her the best advice as an individual. I had to recuse myself from the engagement and ask another planner to take it. I told her, 'I think somebody else could better advise you personally, because I'm still rooting for you guys as a couple."[24] This type of decision making is difficult but necessary. Couple-friendly advisors know when to step out of the engagement and let a trusted colleague take over the account.

In recent years, more advisors are attaining the designation of certified divorce financial analyst (CDFA). These advisors work with individual clients during the divorce proceedings and then refer these clients back to the original couple advisor or another qualified professional once the divorce is complete. This allows the advisor to advocate for the client's best financial interests and also affords the client an opportunity to work with an advisor with specialized training in the legal, technical, and emotional aspects of divorce. This may be a wise option for you if you are in a small or solo practice. For more information about this certification or to find a CDFA in your geographic area, visit their website at http://www.institutedfa.com.

Summary

As a couple-friendly advisor, it is vital for you to understand how couples progress through a series of developmental and family transitions over their lifetime together. By using this knowledge, you can ask more pertinent questions, uncover underlying assumptions, and facilitate a discussion about financial differences and similarities. Clients need your financial and emotional support to navigate life's ups and downs. As a truly client-centric advisor, taking on this role not only is useful for your clients, but can be highly rewarding personally and professionally.

Your Next Step: Dig Deeper with Couple Clients

Make a commitment to learn more about your clients' emotional and developmental stage at your next advisory meeting. Before the meeting, ask yourself the following five questions:

1. What stage of couplehood (i.e., honeymoon, struggle, or acceptance) do I think this couple is in and why?
2. What are the couple's current life circumstances, and where are they in their life span as a couple?
3. How can I help them move smoothly through this transition and possibly anticipate the next?
4. What else do I need to know about their relationship with money and each other to be effective in my role as their advisor?
5. What three questions can I ask at our next meeting to help this couple move forward in their financial and emotional development?

Feel free to create your own questions or use the following questions as a guide. Notice which questions resonate with this couple and which ones fall flat. Make a note of these observations in the file so the next time they meet with you, you can pick up where you left off.

1. What beliefs do you have about love and money?

2. What beliefs does your partner have about love and money?

3. When you are going out together, who pays the bill and why?

4. When do you think it makes sense to start talking about how you would manage money together as a couple?

5. If you have been in a committed relationship before, what would you like to do differently when it comes to money in this new relationship?

6. What is one financial success you would like to share with your partner?

7. What did you learn as a result of this financial success?

8. What is one financial mistake or regret you would like to share with your partner?

9. What did you learn as a result of this financial mistake or regret?

10. If you could ask your partner only one question about his or her relationship to money, what would it be and why?

11. What is your biggest financial concern?

12. What do you perceive is your partner's biggest financial concern?

13. What are your top three life values, and how do you express these in your financial behavior?

14. How are these values the same as or different from your partner's?

15. What financial skills or insights does your partner bring to this relationship that you admire?

16. What is your biggest pet peeve about your partner's financial behavior?

17. On a scale of "1" (lowest) to "5" (highest), how willing are you to accept this financial habit as part of your partner's money personality?

18. What is your biggest pet peeve with your own financial behavior?

19. On a scale of "1" (lowest) to "5" (highest), how willing are you to accept this habit as part of your money personality?

20. If you could change one thing about how you handle your finances as a couple, what would it be and why?

Essential Skills for Couple-Friendly Advisors

6

Build a Solid Foundation

It takes 20 years to build a reputation and five minutes to
ruin it. If you think about that, you'll do things differently.

—Warren Buffett, American self-made billionaire

YOU HAVE ONLY SEVEN SECONDS TO MAKE A GOOD IMPRESSION WHEN
you meet a new couple.[1] In this short time frame, you need to project confidence, demonstrate expertise, and establish yourself as a
trustworthy advisor. To complicate matters, when you are meeting
with a traditional couple, you have to balance the needs of both genders, and if you are meeting with a nontraditional couple, you need
to communicate that you are open to all lifestyles. Often your body
language speaks louder than your words. As you attend to the needs
of each partner, you must also ask open-ended, curious questions to
display that you care. Doing all of these tasks simultaneously is akin
to juggling a set of bowling pins while bouncing on one foot and
reciting the Gettysburg Address. It is challenging.

As with any skill, experience makes facilitating initial couples
meetings easier. You may have been doing this for years and find
it second nature. Or you may be newer to the field and find this
balancing act difficult. Whatever your experience level, it is essential that you know the elements of building a good advisor–couple

client working relationship. These include creating a mission statement that supports your work with couples, identifying and communicating your couples philosophy to your clients, and establishing and fostering trust in every client interaction. Having this clarity and vision about advising couples will take your advisory practice to the next level and ensure that you are truly couple-friendly.

In this chapter, you will tap into what motivates you to do this type of work and use these personal values to craft your advising couples mission statement. You will identify your couples philosophy and learn how to articulate it clearly to your prospects and couple clients. And you will understand the importance of sharing both your couples protocol and your mission statement with clients as a means of building a solid foundation of trust.

Start with the End in Mind

In Stephen Covey's bestselling book *The 7 Habits of Highly Effective People*, his second habit is, "Begin with the end in mind." What he meant was that you need to identify how all your relationships, personal and professional, correspond with your core values and beliefs. Once you do this internal work, then you can write a mission statement. This same principle applies when working with couples. You need to uncover your motivation for advising couples and how this work ties into your core values and beliefs. By doing so, you are in a better position to attract and retain couple clients whom you enjoy advising and to be able to work in a way that resonates with who you are as a person.

To start this process, think about a couple whom you enjoy counseling. Let's call this couple your *ideal couple*. What is gratifying about advising these partners? What draws you to this type of advisor–couple client relationship? What drives you to want to help them financially? With the image of your ideal couple and the answers to these questions in mind, take a moment and circle the words in the following list that you associate with your passion for advising couples. If a word pops into your mind but is not on the list, feel free to substitute it for a word on the list.

Challenge	Communicate	Competition
Conflict	Creativity	Educate
Empathy	Excitement	Facilitate
Fees	Friendship	Growth
Involvement	Leadership	Loyalty
Meaningful	Mediate	Mentoring
Planning	Problem-Solving	Recognition
Religion	Rewarding	Wealth

Next, prioritize the words and select your top three reasons for advising couples. Write these words in the following list and jot down a sentence or two about how each word relates to your work with couples.

Example: Challenge—I enjoy the challenge of getting two partners to hear each other's perspectives about money and investing.

1. _____

2. _____

3. _____

Now, review the statements you just wrote. Based on these insights, write a short paragraph outlining your couples mission statement.

Example: I selected the words Rewarding, Communicate, and Mentoring. My mission is to be a couple-friendly advisor, as I find this work **rewarding** *and I believe good money management is an important component of a marriage/partnership. While this is at times challenging, I like helping couples* **communicate** *about money. My ultimate goal is to be a thought leader in advising couples and eventually* **mentor** *those* *advisors who are junior to me on the skills needed for effectively helping couples plan for their financial lives.*

_____

_____

_____

_____

_____

Post this couples mission statement in your office where you and your staff can easily see it. For the next week, revisit this mission statement and make adjustments where you see fit. Once you feel good about this statement, share it with a few longtime clients and ask them if this is how they experience your work with them. If so, which parts of the mission statement do they see as most evident? If not, what parts of the mission statement do they think you need to do a better job outwardly expressing? Make adjustments in the mission statement based on this feedback.

A couples mission statement is a living, breathing document. Over time, it will shift and change as your skills and your practice grow. It is vital that this statement taps into your personal values and beliefs about the importance of your work. By investing time into figuring out why advising couples is important to you and how you can clearly demonstrate this to your current and prospective clients, you are being purposeful and proactive. As Stephen Covey would say, you are beginning with the end in mind.

Your Couples Protocol

Now that you have crafted your couples mission statement, it is time to develop a protocol for advising couples that matches your mission statement. This protocol, describing how you specifically work with couples, should be clearly defined and spelled out for your clients and your staff. Having a well-thought-out methodology sets the stage for a good working relationship now and for years to come.

Do you already have a process or methodology for advising couples that you routinely follow? Some advisors do, but many do not. If you fall into the latter category, don't worry, because you are not alone. Many advisors see couples but fail to invest the up-front time to carefully decide on their methodology. The result is a reactive approach to advising couples as opposed to a proactive approach. As you know, being proactive in your practice is vital to success over the long term. Therefore, it is important to think through the specifics of your process with couples, what motivates you to practice this way, and how you can communicate this philosophy to your clients.

In His Own Words

I like working with our advisor. He explains things in detail and meets with us at our kitchen table.

—MICHAEL, **44**-YEAR-OLD MARRIED HUMAN RESOURCE DIRECTOR

When I conduct workshops on advising couples, I ask the audience members to line up along an advisor–couple continuum. This continuum ranges from advisors who always meet with a couple together to advisors who meet with only one partner of the couple. Refer to Figure 6.1, Advising Couples Continuum. You are on the right side of the continuum if you require both partners to be present at all meetings and communicate with both members simultaneously. This means that all your e-mails and written correspondence are addressed to both parties. If you are less rigid in your approach and meet regularly with only one partner who is self-selected by

Figure 6.1

Advising Couples Continuum

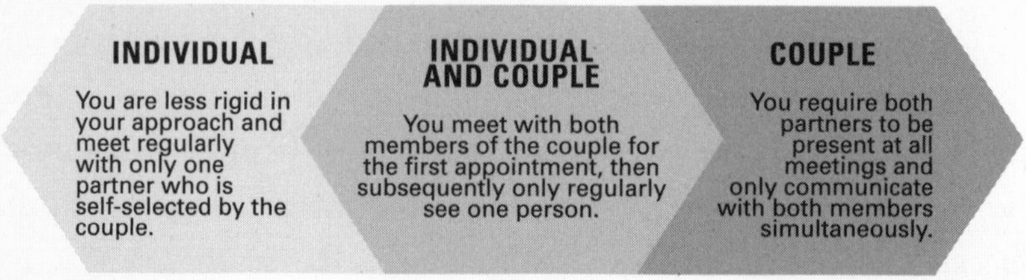

INDIVIDUAL	INDIVIDUAL AND COUPLE	COUPLE
You are less rigid in your approach and meet regularly with only one partner who is self-selected by the couple.	You meet with both members of the couple for the first appointment, then subsequently only regularly see one person.	You require both partners to be present at all meetings and only communicate with both members simultaneously.

the couple, then place yourself all the way at the left end of the continuum. If your style falls somewhere in between, put yourself somewhere in between these two points. For example, if you meet with both members of the couple for the first appointment, then subsequently see only one person regularly, put yourself in the middle of the range. Take a minute to ponder where you are on this advisor–couple continuum. Remember, there are no right answers, just your answer.

Now ask yourself the following questions:

◆ Why do I practice this way?
◆ What contributes to this being my couple-advising style?
◆ How does this serve my clients? How does this potentially get in the way?
◆ How does this serve me as their advisor? How does this potentially get in the way?
◆ What else came to my attention in doing this exercise?

Most advisors meet with couples based on how they were trained or based on the path of least resistance by the couple. The problem with this methodology is that it is not well-thought-out and can inadvertently be a disservice to your clients. You would not design an investment portfolio or a financial plan for a client without putting some time and energy into what makes sense for this client. In the same way, it is vital that you take the time to develop a couples protocol that makes sense for you and your clients.

Based on my experience coaching and training advisors, I have identified three different protocols that advisors use with couples. Each is detailed below.

All or Nothing

The all-or-nothing approach means that your client is the couple and you communicate only with the partners as a unit, no exceptions. All your appointments and correspondence are joint. The rationale behind this service model is that it fosters open communication between the couple and the advisor and minimizes any misunderstandings that can occur if only one partner is involved in a discussion. This approach also helps an advisor avoid the appearance of aligning with one spouse over the other. It ensures that all parties are up to date with the plan and actively involved in the decision-making loop.

The challenge with this model is that it requires the advisor to coordinate schedules with two people rather than one. It also requires the advisor to be adept at balancing both partners' needs in each encounter. As previously discussed in Chapter 1, "The Financial Advisor's Dilemma," this approach calls for more advanced communication skills. However, those who practice this methodology feel the demands are worth the rewards—both for the couple and for the advisor.

Divide and Conquer

This protocol often occurs by default. The advisor meets with one partner, for example, the husband. The advisor may invite the other partner, the wife, for annual meetings, but he or she does not require the wife's involvement as part of the engagement. The advisor's main contact is identified by the couple as the member of the partnership who is better equipped to manage and invest the money. For traditional couples, this typically is the male client. With nontraditional couples, this responsibility often falls to the person with the most financial aptitude and time. Most communication happens unilaterally, and the financially dominant partner speaks for both parties.

The advantage of this model is that it works well for the advisor. It is easier to coordinate schedules with one person than with two. Also, asking probing questions of one person is simpler than interviewing two, as is reaching investment decisions. But be careful because this more traditional service model often results in the nonparticipating spouse feeling left out or, worse yet, neglected by the advisor. In addition, miscommunication can occur even if your main contact is doing his or her best to pass on the other partner's thoughts or questions.

IN HER OWN WORDS

The advisor never once asked if my husband would come with me. He assumed I was the point person, but he never treated us as a couple. I eventually changed advisors.

—*KELLY, 38-YEAR-OLD MARRIED BUSINESS OWNER AND MOTHER OF TWO*

Did you play the game of telephone as a kid? In the old days, this game was played with a series of tin cans tied together with a string. One person whispers something into the can held up to the next person's ear. This person then turns and whispers it to the next person in the line, and so on. This game ends when the person at the end of the chain receives the message and says out loud to the rest of the group what he or she heard. More often than not, the original message became distorted in the process. While this was funny when you were a kid, it is not a laughing matter when financial decisions are involved. Even if nonparticipating spouses do not speak up, know that they are highly likely to move their assets from your book of business at some time in the future, usually when your main contact passes on.

His, Hers, and Ours

This service model mirrors the all-or-nothing approach, but with one big difference. The advisor meets the first time with both members of the couple, then subsequently meets with each individual separately. The purpose of the first meeting is to connect with the couple, observe their couple dynamic, and learn about their shared goals. The follow-up individual appointments are to gather more detailed data on each person's money history, financial literacy, and individual goals. After these individual sessions are held, the couple is strongly encouraged to attend future meetings jointly.

The advantage to this protocol is that the advisor gets an opportunity to solidify the relationship with each partner as well as obtain information that each partner may not be as forthcoming with when meeting jointly. Denise Federer, founder of Federer Performance Management Group, has been coaching advisors for many years on how to work effectively with couples. She states, "There are many marriages where partners *don't* feel comfortable saying the whole truth in front of each other." She recommends that advisors conduct financial history and priorities reviews with each partner after the initial couples meeting. The main purpose of these individual meetings is to understand each partner's money history and identify areas of potential conflict between partners.[2]

It is vital for advisors who use this protocol to be transparent and not keep secrets. If you allow yourself to get caught in the middle of the partners by meeting with them separately, you have fallen into the trap of triangulation discussed in Chapter 3, "Advising and

Couple Dynamics." But when it is done well, this service model helps you establish a strong relationship with each member of the couple, as well as with the couple as a unit.

Ultimately, the mode of operation you select is up to you. It is based on your advising philosophy and your business model. It is also influenced by your training, your compensation structure, and the type of financial services you want to provide.

No matter what your protocol, it is important that you know why you practice this way and how this methodology serves your clients. This couples protocol should be in writing and should clearly articulate the methodology you employ when advising couples. Include specifics regarding who is required to attend fact-finding meetings, financial planning sessions, annual reviews, and periodic check-ins. Specify whom you consult with prior to making any investment and financial decisions, and spell out what, if any, exceptions to these rules of engagement are acceptable. Also include why you choose to practice in this way; clients trust advisors who are transparent and who proactively consider their needs in the advisor–client relationship.

Share this written couples protocol with your clients at their first meeting. Give them a chance to ask questions and then, once both you and your clients are on the same page about how the relationship is going to work, have them each sign a copy. Keep a signed copy in the client folder as well as give a copy to each partner. When you take the time to explain your methodology up front and are transparent about your procedures and expectations, clients can self-select to work with you or not. This gives the clients a chance to opt out if this is not the type of advisory relationship they are looking for. This clarity about your purpose and methods helps you practice more efficiently, as you are not signing on clients who are not a good match for you or your firm.

Crafting this protocol may seem labor intensive, but the real work is following it consistently throughout the client engagement.

Clients inevitably try to break the rules, and you need to reinforce your guidelines. While there may be a tendency to make an exception, it is best to adhere to your original plan. This consistency demonstrates that you believe in your approach. Besides, if the protocol was clearly stated up front, rescheduling or postponing an appointment because only one partner showed up generates a less negative pushback from the couple. Don't forget that technology makes this goal more practical now that one partner can attend by conference call, voice or video, if necessary.

In His Own Words

No matter how strong the couple (appears), make sure both parties are set up financially.
—JEFF, *43-YEAR-OLD MARRIED MANAGEMENT CONSULTANT AND FATHER OF TWO*

If you are committed to better serving female clients, I strongly recommend that your couples protocol require both partners to be present at most, if not all, meetings. Joint communication allows each person to actively participate in the financial decision making, and also communicates to your clients that both viewpoints are important. Furthermore, it minimizes the likelihood of getting caught in the middle of the couple when disagreements about financial and life planning arise or of losing an account when one member of the couple dies unexpectedly.

Following a couples protocol may not always be easy, but it is in the best interest of your clients and your firm. It provides clarity in a process that can sometimes get murky. It also helps you establish trust, as it communicates to your clients that you care enough about them and their money to invest time in developing a system that works.

Building a Solid Foundation of Trust

Clients, especially female ones, know if your words are not congruent with your actions. Therefore, communicating and practicing a philosophy that is tied to your core values is paramount to building a solid foundation of trust with both partners. As you know, trust is at the core of all successful advisor–client relationships. Without it, very little gets accomplished. With it, you can help your couples increase their financial nest egg, improve their financial communication, and assist them in passing on wealth to the next generation.

What is trust? According to the article, "Establishing Trust in the Advisor-Client Relationship," "Trust is defined as a duty, a covenant, a reliance based on faith and confidence."[3] When it comes to trust, an advisor needs to establish both benevolence-based trust and competence-based trust. Benevolence-based trust is the type of goodwill you develop when you show your clients that you care about them and their interests. It is human nature to be more open to trusting someone who is willing to listen to you and shows an interest in what you have to say. This is especially important to female clients. Competence-based trust is a faith in your knowledge and skills in a certain area.[4]

When establishing a relationship with a couple, you need to build both types of trust. According to Laura Varas, principal of Hearts and Wallets LLC, a research firm based in Hingham, Massachusetts, clients trust advisors if they understand how those advisors get paid and the incentives they have to sell certain products. "There's a sense among investors that there's a lot of hidden incentives, like pay-backs and kick-backs . . ." She goes on to share that in their research, the number one factor driving trust is "how the person [advisor] earns money."[5] Other factors such as personal characteristics come into play, but these rank lower than transparency relative to fees. The good news is that this is within your control as an advisor. Take the initiative and discuss your fee structure up front when meeting with a new couple client.

This research rings true with the interviews I conducted with affluent women for my work. One of the biggest complaints these women made about advisors is that they don't listen and they just want to sell you a product. All of them were longing for more benevolence-based trust. Although it is important to be skilled at demonstrating competence and technical expertise for female clients, this often falls short of what is needed to close the deal. They want to know that you put their interests and their family's security ahead of your personal gain. The best way to demonstrate this is to put your clients first and the sale second. Get to know the couple on a deeper level by asking open-ended questions about their values, goals, and emotions related to money. Male clients also appreciate this effort, although for many of them, it is not a game changer.

When establishing trust with individual clients, you need to actively listen to their needs, ask clarifying questions, and reach an understanding of their financial goals and dreams. Establishing trust with a couple is similar; however, it involves building trust with both partners at the same time. You need to factor in gender differences and how each person prefers to connect, communicate, and collaborate in the advisory relationship.

In my book *How to Give Financial Advice to Women: Attracting and Retaining High-Net-Worth Female Clients,* I discuss in great depth how you can build and maintain a good working relationship with your female clients. It begins with an understanding that women often associate the word *wealth* with security.[6] When they consider investing their money with an advisor, they are thinking not only of their own financial security, but also of the well-being of their loved ones. Many women approach the task of hiring a financial advisor similarly to the way they hire a nanny for their children or a caregiver for an elderly parent. They interview several candidates, ask numerous questions, check references, and discuss their findings with their friends and family. Then and only then, do they make a decision to work with you.

While you may experience a woman's hiring process as someone questioning your expertise, she is not. She is just acting as a good wife, mother, and daughter by trying to protect and preserve her family's financial future. Therefore, give the female member of the couple plenty of time to engage in this process and show empathy for her concerns. Whatever you do, don't rush her to make a decision.

IN HER OWN WORDS

I was into the specifics of what we would be investing in, but the advisor wanted to just focus on the amount of money we were going to make in the long term. It was frustrating.

—JENNIFER, 51-YEAR-OLD MARRIED STAY-AT-HOME MOTHER OF TWO

While women often want time and space to make an informed decision, male clients want to size you up quickly based on your expertise. The main question men want you to answer is, "Are you the right guy or gal to help me achieve a high return?" It is not that these men don't want to make sure their family's future is secure; it is just that their litmus test is different from the one used by their wives or female partners.

According to Carol Kinsey Goman, PhD, the author of the *Forbes* article, "Ten Body Language Mistakes Women Leaders Make," men respond more favorably to cues that elicit authority, power, credibility, and status.[7] While there are always exceptions to any gender stereotype, men feel that advisors are trustworthy when they display these traits in their verbal and nonverbal language. You can demonstrate authority by using a firm handshake; maintaining good, straight posture; and speaking in a confident manner. Displaying your credentials and any professional awards on the walls also helps establish yourself as an expert in the field.

How can you balance a female client's need to see you as warm and empathetic and her male counterpart's need to see you as a powerful authority? First, you need to display both benevolence-based and competence-based trust in all your meetings. Next, you need to learn a technique called *balancing the triangle.*[8]

Balancing the Triangle

Have you ever attended a high school or college reunion of a school you did not attend with your significant other? If so, then chances are you know the feelings associated with being left out of the conversation. While the oversight is unintentional, it is probably why you skipped the next reunion and let your partner fly solo. This same phenomenon happens in couples meetings, and when it does, it becomes a barrier to establishing trust with one of the partners. Therefore, you need to be vigilant in balancing the conversation and interactions with each member of the couple from your very first encounter with them.

A simple tool for equalizing your time with each person is shown in Figure 6.2, Balance the Triangle. As you can see, an imaginary triangle connects you and the two partners in a meeting. You are at the top of the triangle, and the partners are at the other two points. The two lines connecting you to the two other points represent your relationship with each of the individuals. The line between the partners represents the dynamic or relationship between the partners. When the triangle is in balance, each individual is participating in the meeting. When the triangle is out of balance, one partner is being left out of the conversation. If the dialogue is out of balance too frequently, then one person, historically the female client, feels ignored or neglected by you, whether this is intentional or not. When this imbalance happens consistently, it blocks the formation of trust or erodes what trust has been established. Just as you decided to opt out of the reunion in the scenario above, the partner who feels neglected often opts out of the appointments going forward.

Figure 6.2

Balancing the Triangle

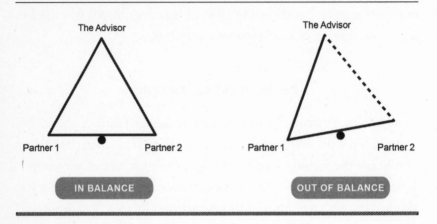

In a typical meeting, the triangle occasionally tips to one side or the other, but it should never be out of balance for too long. Make a point to check in with yourself two or three times during the meeting. Ask yourself silently, "Is the triangle in balance?" If it is not, then consciously redirect the conversation or questioning to the other partner. You can also shift the triangle by adjusting your body posture toward the other partner. Either way, this technique will help even things out.

Summary

It is important that you start any couple engagement with a solid foundation of trust. To do so, you must identify your core values and determine how these tie to your work with couples. Next, you need to establish your couples protocol and follow it consistently throughout the client engagement. This consistency, along with balancing the triangle in meetings, continues to foster trust and loyalty. Working with couples is complex and requires that you adequately prepare by developing protocols and systems. Not only will this help you in developing more mastery in your work, but it also shows respect for the clients you serve.

Your Next Step: Formalizing Your Couples Protocol

Take a moment to consider where you fall on the couples continuum. Refer to Figure 6.1, Advising Couples Continuum. Now place an "x" at the point along the continuum where you see yourself practicing right now. Next, list five factors that motivate you to practice this way. The following is an example of one advisor's list:

Example: *Motivators:*

1. *Both partners need to be at the first meeting.*
2. *The couple gets to decide who is going to be the primary contact, not me.*
3. *It is easier to schedule one person for an appointment.*
4. *I prefer to work with the more financially savvy partner only.*
5. *The male client typically pays my fees.*

Next, review each motivator on the list. Ask yourself, how important is this motivator to my overall advising style? What are the benefits of this motivator to me and to my clients? What are the potential risks associated with this motivator to me and to my clients? For example, the motivator, "The male client typically pays my fees," listed as motivator 5, may be true in your practice, or it may be a faulty assumption. Either way, the benefit to you and to the client is that you get to meet with the more financially savvy partner individually (see motivator 4) and make him happy. The risk associated with this motivator is that it may be the female client who is more economically powerful in the couple, and your misinterpretation of the situation may result in her firing you when she gains full control of the assets through divorce or death.

Once you have examined each motivator and performed a benefit-to-risk analysis, make a conscious decision to stay where you are on the continuum or move in one direction or the other. Also, use this data in developing or fine-tuning your couples philosophy and your couples mission statement, as it is imperative to be consistent with all your couples policies and practices to foster and maintain trust.

7

Balance Gender Differences

> Sometimes I wonder if men and women really suit
> each other. Perhaps they should live next door and
> just visit now and then.

> —Katharine Hepburn, American actress

DARE I SAY IT—GENDER MATTERS? IT IS NOT ALWAYS POLITICALLY correct to say that men and women think, feel, and act differently based on their sex. But there is a good deal of research and life experience that tells me that they do. I have met thought leaders and advisors who believe we should live in a gender-neutral world. In my opinion, this would detract from the beauty of our unique and shared experiences. Like salt and pepper, two genders add a little flavor to life.

As a couple-friendly advisor, you need to be aware of and balance gender differences in your client–advisor relationships. Men and women often view money, wealth, and financial advice differently. With heterosexual couples, this means constantly bridging the gap between what she wants and what he wants. With gay couples, this translates into understanding how two people from the same gender negotiate finances in their partnership. As with any generalization, there are always exceptions to the rule. But one thing is fairly certain: if you don't adjust your style to meet the needs of your female clients, you run a high risk of being fired once their male partners have left the picture.[1]

In my book *How to Give Financial Advice to Women: Attracting and Retaining High-Net-Worth Female Clients,* I discuss how the financial services industry historically has overlooked female clients and offer tips and tools for being more female-friendly. Women clients are highly dissatisfied with the industry and often mistrust advisors.[2] More financial advisors are taking note of female clients as their wealth increases and they realize their economic power both at home and in the workplace. It is true that women control the majority of the wealth in the United States, are starting businesses at twice the national rate, and make 80 percent of the household buying decisions, including whom to hire for financial advice and services.[3–5]

Some financial firms and advisors are working diligently to make female clients feel welcome at the advising table. Others are discounting this opportunity. One thing is for sure: if you are going to advise couples successfully, many of your couples will consist of at least one woman. Therefore, it is imperative for you to reach across the table and welcome your female clients' opinions and viewpoints as much as you do your male clients'. The best method for attracting and retaining women is to understand how the female brain works, how women are socialized differently from men, and how their relationship with money and their advisor may look slightly dissimilar. Let's take a look at each of these areas.

It's All in Your Head

When you are told it is all in your head, it may just be true. The female and male brains are 99 percent the same, but the 1 percent difference is what provides your clients (and you) with a different gender lens.[6] In general, women are hardwired for connection and men are hardwired for individualization. These neurological variations impact how women and men view money, investments, and their financial advisors. It is similar to the difference between Apple and PC computers. Both types of computers provide the user with the same functions, but how they operate and interface is different. Therefore, how you connect, communicate, and collaborate with female versus male clients requires diverse skills. The following chart outlines some key facts about the female and male brains.[7]

The Female Brain

- Ten times more white matter than the male brain
- Connectors in white matter tied to relationship focus, holistic worldview, and multitasking
- Larger limbic system, which may account for women's desire to care for others, at times at their own expense
- Larger hippocampus, which may contribute to women being more detail-oriented than men
- To cope with stress, female brains encourage befriending

The Male Brain

- Six times more gray matter than the female brain
- Gray matter linked to linear thinking and hierarchal decision making
- Fewer connective tissues between brain hemispheres, which results in less verbal access to emotions and feeling states
- Smaller amounts of connective tissue in the corpus callosum, which accounts for single-minded focus
- To cope with stress, male brains encourage fighting

As you can tell from the preceding chart, there are biological reasons why men and women don't always see eye to eye. A classic example of gender differences is the scene that plays out nightly in many homes across the United States. It goes like this: The husband comes home from work and asks his wife, "How was your day?" She tells him about her commute to work, how she got a call from their son's school, about a phone call from her girlfriend, and how now she is worried about her friend's marriage. After about 10 minutes, the wife turns to her husband and asks, "How was your day, honey?" The husband replies, "Fine." The reason this dialogue sounds familiar is that women typically communicate with details and men talk in headlines. Women want and need to verbalize their experiences as if they are sharing a movie plot, one scene at a time. Conversely, men communicate by providing the title of the film. Men don't feel the need to rehash the whole day. Women actually enjoy it.

In addition to the neurological differences between the female and male brain, a person's sex determines how he or she is socialized growing up. Girls traditionally are reared to be "sugar and spice and everything nice," while boys are reared to be "the little men of the house." These societal expectations reinforce some of the biological tendencies that men and women are born with. For example, women learn to define their self-esteem based on how good they are at building and maintaining relationships, and often avoid conflict, as it is not viewed as ladylike. These societal expectations dovetail with their neurological wiring toward connection and collaboration. Conversely, men are expected to be independent and find their self-worth from completing tasks on their own. The male brain supports this individualized, competitive approach to life.

One word of caution: use this information carefully. Women complain when they are pigeonholed into one homogeneous group by financial advisors. Many of these female clients fought long and hard during the Women's Rights Movement to be seen as more than a gender stereotype, so making broad-brush assumptions erodes their trust in you. Male clients also appreciate and benefit when you care enough to not overgeneralize about their experience or their female partner's.

IN HIS OWN WORDS

I think that the sex of the individual is irrelevant. In my relationship, I am the financial leader, not because I am the man, but because I am more adept at handling finances.

—*MICHAEL, 44-YEAR-OLD MARRIED TECHNICAL ALLIANCE MANAGER*

It is hard to tell if our biology dictates our social expectations or if our social expectations influence our biology. I will leave that debate up to the scientists, sociologists, and anthropologists. However, I do believe we may find the answers as society advances and the roles of women and men shift over time. Either these gender variations will remain or they will morph to accommodate a new reality. In the meantime, what is vital for you to understand is how these key gender differences come to life when you are advising couples.

Key Gender Differences

In your work with traditional and nontraditional couples, you need to balance female clients' needs in the advisory relationship with their male counterparts' desires. This is a delicate balancing act, but when it is done well, it creates a strong bond between you and both partners.

The first time you need to factor in these gender differences is during the prospecting and hiring process. In general, men want to work with experts and women want to work with coaches. In fact, men are twice as likely to report that they are interested in achieving the highest return on their investments, whereas women are two times more likely to be interested in holistic financial guidance and planning to meet specific life goals.[8] Neither one of these goals is right or wrong, just different. And they highlight how both clients' gender lenses should be considered when you try to sign on a new couple.

What other areas of your practice should you be concerned with when it comes to balancing gender differences? The answer is, almost all of them. However, the top ones are highlighted in Figure 7.1, Key Gender Differences.

Let's look at three distinct areas you need to master when it comes to balancing key gender differences in advising couples. These are connection, communication, and collaboration.

Figure 7.1

Key Gender Differences

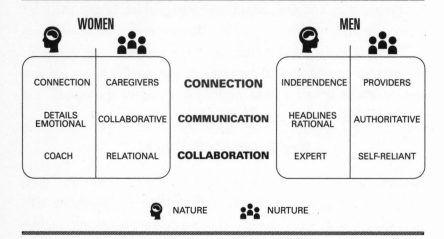

Connection

As previously mentioned, the female brain is hardwired to look for and enjoy relationships. Socially, women are valued for their ability to take care of others. Since cave dweller days, women have relied on intimate relationships for safety, security, and peace of mind. This desire to bond seems to be in a woman's DNA; scans of the female brain show that when women are talking and connecting with others, the pleasure centers of their brains light up. The same is not true for the male brain.

This means that building a relationship with the female member of the couple is paramount. According to the Women of Wealth study conducted by the Family Wealth Advisors Council, 96 percent of the women surveyed "believe it is important for their financial advisors to spend a significant amount of time up-front to understand their entire life picture, not just their finances."[9] While many men also appreciate this effort, they typically don't find it mandatory when working with an advisor. Women do.

> ### IN HER OWN WORDS
>
> *If you want my business, I have to feel connected to you. It's more than just understanding my finances; it's understanding me as your client.*
> —*LAURAN, 44-YEAR-OLD MARRIED ENTREPRENEUR AND MOTHER OF THREE*

In addition to their need to connect, women want advisors who can educate them about money and investments and bolster their financial confidence. Research shows that women, on average, have a lower confidence level when it comes to finances than men. Take a look at a few statistics that support this notion:

- Women are twice as likely as men to describe themselves as financial beginners.[10]
- Forty-eight percent of women agreed with the statement, "Investing is scary for me," which is twice the rate of men who answered this way.[11]
- Ninety percent of women reported feeling insecure when it came to personal finance.[12]

The reason for this lack of confidence is still up for debate. Some experts believe it is a generational phenomenon, with older women being the most affected. Some feel it is a result of the lack of exposure to money management and financial education that women as a group receive. Others postulate that it has more to do with how financial services are delivered. Chances are the answer is a combination of all three of these factors.

I would love to believe that it is an issue specific to women from the traditional and older baby boomer generations, and that in time it will disappear. However, research conducted by Ann Woodyard, PhD, and Cliff Robb, PhD, published in the *Journal of Financial Therapy* in 2012, reports that the most significant gender gaps happen when you compare men and women 18 to 24 years of age and men and women 55 years of age and older.[13] This research highlights that there is still work to be done in getting younger women up to speed when it comes to financial literacy and confidence. Otherwise, this gender gap will remain.

Studies related to men and financial confidence find that, as a gender, they exhibit the exact opposite problem from women. They are too overconfident. In the classic study "Boys Will Be Boys: Gender, Overconfidence and Common Stock Investment," the authors conclude, "Men trade more than women and thereby reduce their returns more so than do women. Furthermore, these differences are most pronounced between single men and single women."[14] This overconfidence leads men to take more risks and chase market returns. Women may be less confident, but they often make better long-term investors because of their cautious nature.

In a recent report by Barclays Wealth, the authors proposed that women avoided riskier investments because of their hormonal makeup. Dr. Emily Haisley, a member of the behavioral finance team at Barclays Wealth, stated, "Biologically, several studies have linked financial risk-taking to testosterone. Emotionally, women tend to experience emotions more strongly than men and are more prone to the experience of fear and anger, both [of] which can make the downside of risk more threatening."[15] Conversely, men view risk positively and experience it as freedom, excitement, and pleasure. While some women are risk takers, their inclination to play it safe with their money may be part of their desire to protect their loved ones now and in the future.

IN HIS OWN WORDS

My mom didn't write a check when my father died. She had a family that was capable and willing to handle her finances for 19½ years. But I didn't want Mom's situation to be duplicated in my female clients' lives, so I do my best to actively involve them in designing their financial future.
—GEORGE MCCUEN, FOUNDER AND PRESIDENT OF NAPA WEALTH MANAGEMENT

It is important to realize that women's collective lack of financial confidence and their tendency to be more risk averse does not mean that they do not want to be involved in their family finances.[16] They simply want to find advisors who understand their unique financial problems as women and can work with them and their partners to find workable solutions. They also want someone who will factor in their confidence and risk-tolerance level along with their significant other's and help facilitate a financial planning solution that addresses these sometimes conflicting desires.

Part of finding a solution that works for women is realizing how their relationship to wealth may be different from that of their male partners. Women associate money and the accumulation of wealth with security for themselves and their families, whereas men view wealth as a source of power and status.[17] When it comes to passing on wealth, women want to make sure they are not a burden to their children, and men want to leave a legacy.[18] In the same way that women want you to see them holistically, they want you to appreciate their holistic view of money and their role as caregiver.

This is not to say that women don't want to realize good returns. Instead, they see their investments and the associated risk as a way to achieve real-life goals, such as paying for their child's college education, funding their business endeavor, or covering the cost of their parent's eldercare. Men may want to use money in the same way, but they tend to see money in a more compartmentalized fashion. This is probably a result of their male brains being more single-task-focused and of years of being told that the man who dies with the most toys wins.

The last factor to consider when connecting with female clients is their desire to see you as an authentic person. In the feminine world, showing your vulnerabilities to another person is seen as a strength, not a weakness. It fosters trust and levels the playing field. In the masculine world, however, showing your weaknesses is viewed as dangerous and ill-advised. In a man's world, trust is built by establishing yourself as top dog and proving that you can get the job done. As you can imagine, this is a dilemma when prospecting for and advising couples. She wants you to be real. He wants you to be the best. My suggestion is to be both. Show her your authentic side by having pictures of your family on your desk, telling a story or two that she can relate to, and being transparent about your challenges. And show him that you are good at what you do and you will work hard to achieve a good return on his behalf. Chances are, if you accomplish this balance, your female client will appreciate your honesty and your male client will appreciate your effort to connect with his partner and demonstrate expertise.

Communication

To be a couple-friendly advisor, you must understand how to read verbal and nonverbal communication as well as be aware of gender differences in communication styles. Verbal communication is defined as using words and language to send a message. Nonverbal communication is defined as using body language and gestures to convey meaning. Let's take a look at each type of communication and how men and women can differ in this area.

First of all, do women really talk more than men? If you asked a group of husbands, they probably would give a resounding "yes!" However, there is conflicting research on this topic. For years, it was widely reported that women speak 20,000 words a day, whereas men speak only 7,000. In 2007, researchers at the University of Arizona published a study that debunked this finding. They found that women and men verbalize about the same amount in a day. In their study, women used 16,215 words a day and men used 15,669.[19] In life, I know women (myself included) who are "highly verbal" and men who are "chatty." So it is less about how often a man or a woman speaks up and more about how he or she prefers to communicate and be communicated with that is important.

The women I interviewed for this and previous books tell me that they trust advisors who actively listen and pay attention to their feelings as well as their words. This is not surprising to me because there is evidence that the female brain is wired to have a greater access to emotions and a greater proclivity toward verbalizing feelings feelings than the male brain.[20] This hardwiring translates into a woman's desire to have an advisor who is willing to pay attention to the emotional and human side of finance. For example, if a grandmother shares with you and her husband that she is interested in saving for her granddaughter's education, it would be prudent to ask her how providing a college education for her grandchild might feel and what motivates her toward this goal. While your tendency may be to jump into a lecture about 529 plans, it is best to slow down and ask more feeling-oriented questions first, as women want to feel understood before you offer concrete solutions. Of course, verbalizing thoughts and feelings related to financial decisions is useful for most clients, but with women it is a paramount step toward building and maintaining trust.

Next, it is important to know that women generally use collaborative language when they are talking with other people. Collaborative language is marked by words such as *we*, *ours*, and *us*. Not surprisingly, the feminine desire to connect and relate contributes to this preference. Conversely, men use authoritative language, which is more hierarchal in nature. They tend to use words such as *I* and *me*, which speak to their individualized perspective. Because women tend to find authoritative language dismissive, it is best for you to err on the side of using collaborative language in a couples meeting. This shows the female client that she is an important part of the financial team and minimizes any competitive tendencies the male client may be prone to if you use a more masculine approach.

IN HER OWN WORDS

He calls it his *money. It drives me crazy.*
—*MARY, 64-YEAR-OLD MARRIED WOMAN WITH TWO ADULT CHILDREN*

In addition to the language you use in a meeting, it is important to ask your clients how they prefer to communicate with you in general. You can do this by asking direct questions or using an assessment tool. The simplest approach is to directly ask each partner these three questions:

1. How does each of you prefer to receive data?
2. How do you prefer to receive correspondence outside the meetings (phone, e-mail, text, or snail mail)?
3. What type of learner (visual, auditory, or kinetic) are you?

There are also online tests, some of which are free of charge and others that are offered through a monthly subscription, which you can use to assess your clients' communication styles. As one advisor shared with me, this type of assessment dramatically changed her practice: "Now I discuss their individual communication preferences in the first meeting, and I share my test results with them as well. Since instituting this protocol, I close more accounts and retain more clients. It has even helped me communicate better with my husband!"

Verbal communication is a vital piece of the advisory relationship puzzle, but often, the most powerful form of communication is nonverbal in nature. Clients are reading your nonverbal communication from the second they enter your office. They notice if you look them in the eye, stand with confidence, or shake their hand firmly. For this reason, you need to be cognizant of your body language and what it is communicating to your female and male clients.

In Her Own Words

It is my responsibility as a financial advisor to speak in a language that both female and male clients understand. It is important to check in with both spouses to make sure both comprehend the information.

—KAREN SARTEN, VICE PRESIDENT, BEACON POINT ADVISORS

Akin to how there is a gender variance when it comes to verbal communication, there are certain gestures that translate differently to a woman versus a man. In general, women display body language that conveys warmth to the other person. For example, head tilting is more of a feminine posture that demonstrates listening. Women also tend to use body language that expresses empathy, likability, and caring. Men display nonverbal communication that is more authority driven. For example, a man often takes up a fair amount of physical space in a room, which indicates status, power, and credibility.[21] Next time you are in a work setting and a group of men and women sit down at a conference table, notice who positions him- or herself at the head of the table. Often it is a man.

Last year I was asked to present to a group of lawyers as part of their women's initiative. The group was made up of approximately 35 women and 5 men, all at about the same professional experience level. During the program, I invited the audience to participate. I was struck by the fact that most of the men spoke up, but only one of the women voiced her opinion. After the presentation was over, I turned to the group organizer and wondered about this out loud. She had noticed the same phenomenon; however, when the group included only women, the female professionals who had acquiesced to the men spoke freely.

This experience speaks to the feminine inclination to wait to be asked to speak up. It is a tendency that often gives the impression that women have nothing to contribute. But the reality is that women are just politely waiting for permission to give their two cents' worth. Remember this the next time you are in a financial meeting and are buying into the idea that because the female partner is silent, she is not interested. Chances are she is just listening and waiting to be asked a question.

The other gesture commonly misread by advisors is nodding. When a man nods in a meeting, he is agreeing with what is being said. When a woman nods, she is listening to the communication but not necessarily agreeing with the content. As a woman, I know this to be true, and I am always struck by how fascinating and eye-opening my male advisor friends find this tidbit. It is a great example of how a simple body movement can be so easily misread based on your gender.

The bottom line is, women and men read body language differently. As an advisor, it is important to look a female client directly in the eye and to maintain an open posture. This conveys trustworthiness. The easiest way to do this is to seat the female member of the couple directly across from where you are sitting during the meeting. It is best to seat the male client at a slight angle to where you are positioned. This reduces the masculine tendency toward competitiveness and establishes you as the expert in the room. While these nuances may seem small, they can make a big difference in the tone and effectiveness of your couples meetings.

Collaboration

As previously mentioned, women want to collaborate with their financial advisors and their partners when it comes to financial planning and decision making. This desire to connect and talk through their options can be misconstrued as a lack of confidence or as a direct challenge to the authority of an advisor. However, this wish to ask questions and learn through dialogue is just the way women process information. Think back to the days when people lived on the prairie. At night the women would gather round the fireplace and sew and knit together. While they were being industrious, they also were satisfying their need to learn about the world through conversation. The upside of this gender preference is that it makes women more consultant-friendly, once trust is established. This is also why women's groups and seminars can be so successful in obtaining new female clients. The downside is that you may have to extend your meeting time to accommodate a woman's need to connect in this way.

When it comes to decision making, men often prefer a more unilateral approach. This may be partly because the male brain sees a problem, then fixes the problem, whereas the female brain sees a problem, talks about the problem, then talks more about the problem, then works together with her friends and family to find a solution. Again, neither method is right or wrong, just distinctly different.

IN HER OWN WORDS

In the end, we always have the same goal, but we may arrive at that goal in very different ways. Neither of which is wrong, they're just different.

—*STEPHANIE, 39-YEAR-OLD DIVORCED AND REMARRIED PROFESSIONAL AND*

MOTHER OF FIVE

For some men, the tendency to act unilaterally contributes to him dominating the couples meeting. This is especially true with older couples who generationally believe it's the man's job to manage the money. While this may work for him, it is a slippery slope, as his female partner may not feel attended to by you. To combat this meeting dilemma, try these steps. First, calmly and politely ask the male partner to let his partner speak. Simply say, "It is so helpful to hear where you stand on this issue, and I would also like to hear from your wife. Would it be okay if we took a few minutes to have her answer the same question?" By asking for permission, you are allowing the dominant partner, in this scenario the man, to save face and remain in control, while at the same time opening the door for the non-dominant partner to speak up.

Next, if the male client responds by stating that he can talk for both of them, take a minute to educate the couple about the importance of each partner giving his or her perspective on the financial matter at hand. In a non-judgmental tone, make the following statement, "You are excellent at speaking for the couple on financial matters, and I appreciate your insight and input. With all my couples, I want to hear from both partners, even if they both say the same thing. This does two things. First, it allows me to make sure all three of us are on the same page and understand the plan or recommendation fully. Second, it helps me develop a relationship with both partners in case an unfortunate event occurs and you are too sick or for some other reason can't attend meetings, and your partner is left to manage the money. Would it be okay to proceed with a few questions for your partner based on these concerns?"

Again you are giving the dominant client a sense of control by asking permission, but you are also adding some information about why it is important for you to have a relationship with both individuals. Some men measure their self-worth by their ability to take care of their wives financially. Therefore, if you reframe his letting her talk in meetings as taking care of her financially, he may be more receptive to the idea. And if he still declines, you have sent a clear message that you are open to collaborating with her as well.

Incorporating gender differences into each couples meeting is more art than science. You need to first find out how each member of the partnership prefers to relate to you and develop a relationship with each partner based on these preferences. Next, you must discover how each client prefers to communicate both inside and outside of the office and go out of your way to accommodate their styles. Lastly, you should allow enough time for the female partner to verbalize her concerns, tell her story, and ask her questions during the meetings. While her male partner may not need this type of attention, it is prudent to offer her this extra time. Not only is the female client often the one who makes the majority of the household buying decisions, but in the modern couple, she is highly likely to have real economic power behind her.

Your Gender and Advising Couples

You may be wondering how your gender impacts your ability to attract and work with couples and female clients. The answer is, it depends—on your clients' experience and your ability to adjust your advising style to meet the needs of both partners. If you are a male advisor, your preferences for communicating, learning, and interacting may be different from your female clients' preferences. However, if you practice good client-centric services, you can adjust your advising style to meet the needs of the couple's partnership, not your own. Also, there is no evidence that female clients want to work only with female advisors. In fact, most women are more concerned with the advisor's competence, trustworthiness, and transparency than with gender. The exception is widows and divorced women; one out of every four of these clients prefers to work with another woman.[22]

If you are a female advisor, don't overrely on your ability to connect and socialize. While this is a strength, the mistake most women advisors make is not spending enough time sharing their expertise with the couples. No matter what gender you are, there are pros and cons to it and traps to look out for.

The best course of action its to be knowledgeable and aware of the gender differences in the couple and in the advisor relationship. Notice when you might need to adjust your style to better match how your couples want to connect, communicate, and collaborate. And when in doubt, ask.

Summary

As a couple-friendly advisor, you need to be aware of and balance gender differences in your client–advisor relationships. You have discovered that men and women can view money, wealth, and your role in their life differently. It is vital to your success in working with both traditional and nontraditional couples that you work to bridge the gap between genders, while at the same time avoiding overgeneralizations. At times, this can be like walking a tightwire, but with knowledge and practice, you can master this feat.

Your Next Step: Gender Boot Camp

Every year my husband and his ski buddies head up north to our condo to ski together. When the snow is good, I jump on board as an honorary "guy." (Don't worry; some years I give them their privacy.) What these experiences have taught me is how much what I study about gender holds true in real life. These men do connect and communicate differently from my female friends. I always enjoy this time with them and always look forward to a good long chat with a girlfriend when I return.

To learn more about the opposite sex, I recommend that you put yourself through a self-designed gender boot camp. This may involve crashing a girls' weekend or tagging along on a guys' night out. Of course, you need permission from all the members of the group to attend because your presence will shift the dynamic slightly. But if everyone is agreeable, then you get a chance to see how groups of women versus groups of men interact.

The following is a gender-specific checklist to bring with you on your adventure.

Gender Boot Camp Checklist
For Men

___ Observed use of collaborative language such as "we," "our," and "us"
___ Observed tendency to talk in details
___ Observed connecting through sharing stories and vulnerabilities
___ Observed use of feeling-oriented words
___ Observed bonding when sharing with each other

Other observations: _____

_____

For Women

___ Observed use of authoritative language such as "I" and "me"
___ Observed tendency to talk in headlines
___ Observed connecting through verbal sparring and one-upmanship
___ Observed use of rational, factual language
___ Observed bonding through physical activities such as sports

Other observations of note: _____

_____

Do you prefer a less experimental approach? Read the following books based on your gender. For men, I highly recommend *The Female Brain* by Dr. Louann Brizendine; *Knowing Your Value: Women, Money and Getting What You're Worth* by Mika Brzezinski; and *The End of Men: And the Rise of Women* by Hanna Rosin. For women, I highly recommend *The Male Brain* by Dr. Louann Brizendine; *Men Are from Mars, Women Are from Venus* by John Gray; and *The Male Factor: The Unwritten Rules, Misperceptions, and Secret Beliefs of Men in the Workplace* by Shaunti Feldhahn.

8

Uncover Money Mindsets

Tell me and I forget. Teach me and I remember.
Involve me and I learn.

—Benjamin Franklin, eighteenth-century statesman, scientist, and writer

WHEN I WAS A LITTLE GIRL, I LOVED MY TOY CASH REGISTER. I LOVED the "ka-ching" sound it made when the cash drawer opened and the bright red color, and I loved counting the shiny coins inside. My first money memory is sitting on the floor playing and giggling each time the toy rang out loud. If this had been my only financial memory, my relationship with money would have been simple: I liked the sound, touch, and feel of it, and I wanted more. But like all of us, I grew up and had many experiences with money. Some of these memories are joyful; others trigger a sense of shame. By the time I was in my thirties and married, these money messages were deeply ingrained in my psyche but did not reside in my conscious thoughts. Every time I bought a new pair of boots, I felt guilty but was uncertain why. Each time my husband would generously pick up the check for the entire group at a restaurant, I would feel angry but confused by the intensity of my feelings. My money mindset was fully developed, but I was unaware of how it impacted my financial thoughts and behaviors.

It was not until my husband and I faced our biggest financial challenge that I started to examine my thoughts and beliefs about money. Prior to losing tens of thousands of dollars to an unscrupulous contractor, I firmly believed that my way of interacting with money was the right way—end of story. But what I discovered through this financial betrayal was that my way was just my way. Sometimes it served me. Sometimes it did not. My husband had another set of experiences with money, and his thoughts and feelings were different, but not wrong. It took losing a large sum of money and facing the fear of not having enough to pay the bills for me to figure out that I had some unhealthy messages about money. For a former commissioned FDIC bank examiner, this was a tough admission. But it was the start of open and honest communication between my husband and me about money. This crisis resulted in the greatest gift. We started talking openly about finances and sharing our money histories. We found out that learning each other's thoughts and feelings about finances strengthened our marriage. It made my guilt around spending and his desire to lavish others with gifts make sense. With this increased insight, we were able to financially plan for the future and manage money without pointing fingers. It taught me that you don't have to be perfect around money, just open to learning as you go.

How can you help your couples identify their money thoughts and beliefs before a crisis erupts? By teaching them how to uncover the money scripts that together make up their money mindset. A money script is a thought, belief, or attitude toward money that you learned by observing your parents and other influential adults interact with money. If you were lucky, your parents also taught you overtly about money management. However, many adults did not receive this type of financial literacy training and were left to their own interpretation of events to form their money scripts. They are called *money scripts* because in the same way as an actor reads a script and is instructed on how to play a scene, a money script dictates how you act in a financial situation. Ultimately, these scripts impact your saving, spending, giving, and investing habits on a daily basis. The tricky part is that money scripts often reside in your unconscious mind; therefore, you do not recognize the effect they have on your financial habits and decision making.

The other problem with money scripts is that they are primarily developed during childhood, at a time when you don't have the developmental capacity to fully appreciate the complexities of money and wealth. Therefore, these beliefs are oversimplified. For example, you may have witnessed your mother smiling each time she deposited money into her bank account. As a result, you developed the money script "Saving money is good." While on the surface this is a healthy financial belief, it can be troublesome when the financially wise decision is to incur debt. Because your child's mind says "Saving money is good," by simple logic, it would follow that "Borrowing money is bad."

This all-or-nothing thinking is often what gets clients into trouble when managing money. The two people in front of you act like adults and talk like adults, but they think about money like children. It is not until you help them uncover their money scripts and decide as mature adults which messages to keep and which ones to let go of that they can make more well-informed financial decisions.

IN HER OWN WORDS

As a young girl, my uncles would offer a few bucks to me and the other nieces and nephews if they could spray us with the freezing cold water from the garden hose. Looking back, I see that this is where I learned that money equals pain.

—STACEY, *39-YEAR-OLD MARRIED COMMUNICATIONS CONSULTANT AND AUTHOR*

It is part of the role of a couple-friendly advisor to assist couples in identifying, understanding, and discussing the money scripts that make up their money mindsets. Not only does this help the couples engage in more productive financial discussions and set more realistic financial goals, but it helps them view you as a trusted advisor. In a study conducted by the *Journal of Financial Planning* aimed at examining what activities engender more trust in clients than others, the authors found that clients most value financial advisors with these skills. They discovered that clients want advisors who explore and learn about their experiences, cultural expectations and bias, money personalities, and family histories and values.[1] While this type of exploration gets labeled as the "soft side" of finance by some in the industry, it is highly valued by clients and should be part of your work with couples.

Before learning how to tap into your clients' money mindsets, let's take a look at how a person's money scripts and attitudes are formed.

The Making of a Money Mindset

A variety of factors contribute to clients' money mindsets. These include their family money messages, socioeconomic status, gender, age, religion, culture, and personal financial experiences. Let's look at each one briefly.

Family Money Messages

How your parents and caregivers handled financial matters during your childhood greatly affects your financial decision making as an adult. If your parents fought about money constantly and worked three jobs to make ends meet, you probably considered money scarce and talking about it difficult. However, if you grew up in a family with plenty of resources and your parents talked calmly about money, you may find managing money pleasurable. These early childhood experiences, especially those between 5 and 14 years of age, form the majority of your money scripts and influence your financial habits daily.

In Her Own Words

My father is mostly opposite my mother with regard to money. I can recall him saying things like, "Don't worry, kids; if you forget something, we will just buy a new one" and "Let's shop until we drop." Mom was clearly the disciplinarian, and Dad gave us whatever we wanted.

—*Jennifer, 29-year-old married professional*

Money messages also are passed down from generation to generation. These financial legacies are seldom overtly communicated to the next generation, but instead are a result of observed behaviors. Family members are then left to interpret these habits as scripts of their own. One sibling can view mom and dad working hard as admirable, while another sees it as shameful. Depending on the interpretation, the individual siblings develop different financial beliefs and habits. The goal of your work with couples is to help them identify these family money messages, communicate them to their partners, and together decide which beliefs serve them and which should be left behind.

Socioeconomic Status

The socioeconomic status of your family of origin contributes to how you think and feel about money. Clients who grew up in lower socioeconomic classes have different money scripts from those who were raised in financially privileged homes. According to Brad Klontz, PsyD, and Ted Klontz, PhD, authors of *Mind over Money*, common money scripts for clients from impoverished backgrounds include the following:[2]

- ◆ "If one of us makes it, they owe the rest of us a hand up."
- ◆ "If we get it, we need to spend it before it is taken away from us."
- ◆ "There will never be enough."
- ◆ "Wealthy people got that way by taking advantage of people like us."

All these money beliefs encourage scarcity thinking and often result in these individuals thinking that they are not empowered to change their financial situations. While clients from upper-income families often have different money scripts, they still can be problematic. As the Klontzes say, "Contrary to popular belief that having more money makes you happier, anxiety about money often increases proportionately with net worth; the more a person has, the more they are afraid of losing it."[3] As I discussed in my book *How to Give Financial Advice to Women*, affluence can feel like a weight or a burden. Therefore, it is important to ask open-ended questions about clients' socioeconomic backgrounds and not make assumptions based on your preconceived notions of social class.

Gender

Our clients' money mindsets are also impacted by their gender. While the expectations may vary from culture to culture, boys and girls are reared with different societal money messages. In the United States, boys are raised to be competitive, to make money, and to be good providers for the family. Girls are taught to be good caregivers, to be emotionally supportive to others, and to put their financial wants and needs second to the needs of those around them. While these traditional gender roles are shifting in the modern family, the money messages associated with gender run deep. I have coached many accomplished women who secretly struggle to ask for a fair wage at work, deposit money into their retirement fund if it means fewer resources for their children, or put their financial dreams aside to support those of their partners. Even if you were brought up to believe that men and women are financial equals, there is often still a tendency to buy into the idea that men are better at and more interested in finance than women. Unfortunately, many in the financial services industry perpetuate this myth by catering primarily to male wealth creators at the expense of their female partners.

IN HER OWN WORDS

As a little girl, I was taught by my mother that money equaled happiness. Every weekend we would go to the mall and shop our cares away.

—SHEENA, 52-YEAR-OLD MARRIED GRAPHIC DESIGNER

When advising couples, ask each partner, "What gender money messages did you learn growing up?" "How do these gender money beliefs impact how you think, feel, and act around money in your couplehood?" and "How do these gender money messages serve you versus get in the way financially?" When spouses' or partners' views on gender and money align, there is often less conflict in their financial lives. However, when they are vastly different or have evolved over time, it is vital to their financial health that these scripts are brought to the surface and discussed.

Age

The generation your clients belong to colors their perspectives about money and wealth. For example, a female client in her seventies from the traditionalist generation, defined as those born before 1946, is most likely frugal and apt to defer financial decisions to her husband. This client has lived through the Great Depression, and World War II, and knows what it means to save before you spend.

Conversely, a female client in her twenties from the millennial generation, defined as those born after 1982, is more likely to use credit cards to make purchases and believe in financial equality when it comes to financial decision making in couplehood. For most of her life, she lived in a time of prosperity and economic growth. Reared by baby boomer parents, she was taught that she could have or be anything, regardless of her sex. Neither client's viewpoint is wrong, just influenced by the time period in which they grew up and the generational milestones of their respective eras. So keep generational differences in mind when examining clients' money mindsets.

Religion

Religion and money have an interesting, sometimes strained relationship. No matter what your religious upbringing or current affiliation, religion has a bearing on your money scripts. For example, the biblical scripture that states, "The *love of* money is the root of all evil," has had a powerful effect on Christians and how they view wealth versus poverty. In Christianity, it is noble to be poor. Conversely, in Judaism, the accumulation of wealth is not evil so long as wealth is used wisely. When you are interviewing a couple, it is important to understand how their religious and spiritual beliefs impact their financial attitudes and practices. Over the years, I have coached many individuals whose religious beliefs played a major role in their financial lives. Therefore, it is important to ask your couple clients about this factor and how they see it impacting their spending, saving, and gifting habits.

IN HIS OWN WORDS

I am ambiguous about money. It's never been my goal to make money. If I had more money, I'd just give it away.

—*PAUL, 60-YEAR-OLD DIVORCED MINISTER AND FATHER OF TWO*

Culture

Like religion, clients' cultures contribute to their money mindsets. For clients who grew up in the mainstream consumer-driven U.S. economy, messages such as "the man who dies with the most toys wins" and "spend now, save later" run rampant. Buying items on credit is commonplace, and maintaining a balance on a credit card or having a large mortgage loan on your house is not unusual. However, in other cultures, such as China and Japan, debt is seen as something to avoid and, at its extreme, shameful. Asian clients may not want to rely so much on debt to fund their dreams, but instead focus on good old-fashioned savings. For Latino clients, financial responsibility is about not just paying one's own way, but financially supporting the entire family. The nuances of culture and how they influence individual clients and couples make it vital for you to inquire about cultural backgrounds and the prevailing money messages embedded in them.

Personal Experiences

Personal money experiences, whether viewed as positive or negative, impact clients' money scripts. Significant events such as winning the lottery, receiving a sizable inheritance, filing for bankruptcy, going through an expensive divorce, or being laid off leave a lasting mark on money psyches and, ultimately, alter money beliefs. Each of these events comes with a variety of mixed emotions that need to be understood and eventually integrated into clients' money mindsets. During the global financial crisis in 2008, many clients experienced personal financial traumas such as losing jobs, houses, and life savings. Therefore, you need to inquire about the impact of this recent event as well as others from their past to uncover any hidden scars. These experiences, while often hidden from view, contribute to how clients see their relationship with money, their ability to take care of themselves and their families financially, and you.

In His Own Words

Time spent planning your financial future together is time very well spent.

—*RICO, 46-YEAR-OLD MARRIED ENGINEER AND FATHER OF THREE*

As you can see, there are many facets to clients' money mindsets. For couples with diverse upbringings, it is important to discuss how their respective experiences contribute to their values and habits. For couples with similar family backgrounds, the differences in money mindsets might be less glaring, but still present. Helping your couple clients bring their money scripts to the surface and consciously decide how to operate as a partnership financially is an important service. This sets the stage for open and honest communication about money between the couple, as well as with you as their advisor.

Tools for Tapping into Clients' Money Mindsets

There are many tools for uncovering clients' thoughts and beliefs about money. They range from straightforward questionnaires to highly researched personality tests. In the following sections are detailed descriptions of four tools: money questionnaires, money-o-grams, money personality tests, and money style indicators. Each has its advantages and drawbacks, so select the format that works best for you, your clients, and your practice.

Money Questionnaires

The first assignment given to my graduate students at Bentley University is the completion of a money questionnaire. This questionnaire asks them about their first money memory; the effect of their parents on their saving, spending, investing, and giving habits; and how their personal experiences with money might impact their effectiveness with clients. This questionnaire is often the assignment that students enjoy the most. It offers them valuable insights into their relationship with money and how their money mindsets impact their advising style and effectiveness. It also helps them explore the emotional side of finances and assists them in identifying blind spots and biases that may positively or negatively shape their work with clients.

Asking your clients to complete a money questionnaire similar to the one I use in my class is an easy way to gather this important data. It also gives you and your couple clients a framework for talking about the emotions behind financial decisions. As part of your work to become a highly skilled, couple-friendly advisor, I encourage you to complete the questionnaire as well. It is included in the "Your Next Step" section at the end of this chapter. While there are many forms of this type of money questionnaire, I find this 20-question, sentence-completion format to be useful. Feel free to use my questionnaire, to create your own survey, or to adapt what you see other professionals doing to suit your purposes.

Money-O-Grams

One of my favorite tools for capturing money messages is called the *money-o-gram*. The money-o-gram is based on a map called a *genogram* that is used in the psychological field. It looks a lot like a family tree, and it is used by mental health professionals to keep track of family relationship patterns across generations. In financial advising, this tool is a visual representation of the couple and their extended family's values and money scripts and often goes back three generations. An example of a completed money-o-gram is shown in Figure 8.1, money-o-gram.

As you can see from Figure 8.1, which is a money-o-gram of my family, I come from a long line of savers. Government jobs and security were key money messages in my family of origin, and these ran across generational lines. My maternal grandfather, John Sr., worked for a public school, and my mother followed suit by working first as an elementary school teacher, then as a town librarian. My paternal grandfather, Bill Sr., was an outlier in the family as he loved gambling

Figure 8.1

Money-O-Gram

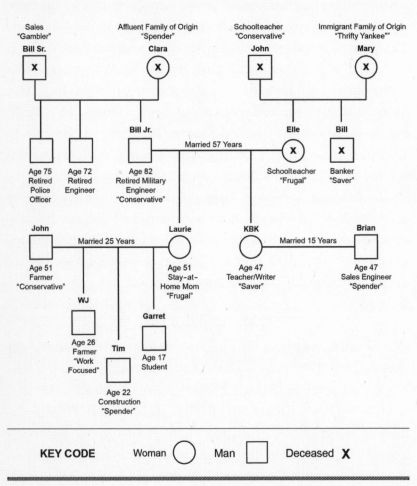

KEY CODE   Woman ◯   Man ▢   Deceased **X**

and worked several jobs over his career. My father, Bill, is overly conservative in his spending and saving habits in response to the financial uncertainty in his childhood. He joined the Navy and had a secure paycheck for 27 years. He then worked for a public school system for another 15 years. My mother, Eleanor, a stay-at-home mother and thrifty Yankee, learned how to save from her mother.

Nana Mo, as we called her, was the queen of Filene's Basement, a famous Boston department store known for its bargains. My sister, Laurie, and I are both savers, but when it came to husbands, we picked opposite money personalities. Laurie's husband, John, is a farmer who works for a state college, whereas my husband, Brian, is a salesman type who enjoys spending money on the finer things in life. My entrepreneurial spirit comes from my paternal grandfather and is balanced out with a healthy dose of conservatism from my father. Time will tell how these money beliefs and values will trickle down to my nephews and eventually their children.

I share my family's money-o-gram with you as I believe it is important for any professional working with clients around money and wealth to have some insight into his or her own relationship with money and be open about it. I encourage you to complete your own money-o-gram as a way to master this tool and gain insight into your money personality. Besides, it can be fun to find out what values and scripts have been passed down generationally.

IN HER OWN WORDS

The genogram (money-o-gram) has helped me in knowing how to approach clients, when to approach them, and having the clients feel that I care about them and their next generations. It helps deepen the relationship as well as assists us in understanding the psychological aspects of wealth transfer. It can have an exponential effect in client satisfaction and retention.

—CANDY L. BOBONIS, SENIOR VICE PRESIDENT, BOBONIS, OCHOA & FULLANA GROUP

Here are the steps for completing a money-o-gram and the procedures to use, whether you are doing this activity for yourself or with your clients.

Step 1: Map Out Your Family Structure

The first step is to map out your family tree. Use a square to symbolize each male and a circle to symbolize for each female. A horizontal line is used to show a married or committed couple, and a horizontal line with two hash marks in it represents a divorced couple. Children are drawn below their parents with vertical lines, indicating this parent–child relationship. To keep it simple, if they are stepchildren from a previous marriage or relationship, or adopted or foster children, just note this on the chart. Line up the siblings from firstborn on the left to last born on the right. Often, it is easiest to start by drawing your client couple and their immediate family, then going up one generation at a time.

Step 2: Fill in Specifics

Now that the family structure is mapped out, it is time to fill in the details. For each family member, ask the following questions:

◆ What is each person's name, age, and occupation?
   Note this on the money-o-gram. For relatives who are
   deceased, write down the age at which they died and,
   if relevant, the cause of death and any inheritance or
   debt left for the next generation.
◆ What is known about each person's money scripts or
   beliefs? Jot down the overarching money belief of each
   individual. For example, in my money-o-gram, my
   father has many values and beliefs related to money,
   but his overall money personality is conservative;
   therefore, it is noted as such next to his name.
◆ What financial conflicts have there been in the family, if
   any? Jot down the conflict between the parties and some
   key words to capture the essence of the disagreement.

◆ What money values have been passed down from previous generations, and by whom? Which of these values would you like to pass down to the next generation? Write down these values next to the person or the couple to whom these lessons are attributed, and note which ones the couple is interested in passing on.

◆ What else do you think is important to know about your family when it comes to money? Write down this additional information as you see fit.

There are many more questions you could ask and data you could gather, but the preceding inquiries give you the basic information needed to facilitate a conversation about money scripts and family money patterns.

Step 3: Ask the Couple to Review the Money-O-Gram Between Appointments

This step allows the couple to take a copy of the money-o-gram that was completed in the meeting home with them. They can review it at their leisure, fill in blanks as they learn more information, or use it as a tool to talk more openly about money with of their members extended family. The goal is for them to digest this information and bring back the completed money-o-gram to the next session. Be careful not to skip over this step. Often the most useful information is discovered when the clients are not in your office.

Money-o-grams capture a large amount of data in a concise manner and make it easy to reference this information going forward. Also, the act of creating this document with your couple clients involves them in the process of learning about their money history and how their mindsets developed over time. This co-creation builds and fosters trust among the three of you and is a great tool for revisiting these concepts in the future.

Money Personality Testing

There are a variety of money personality tests available for advisors to use with clients. These assessments are validated, and some, such as the Moneymax Money Personality Profile and Financial DNA, specifically look at a client's attitudes toward money, risk, and investing. Two other popular tests, the Kolbe A Index and the Myers-Briggs Type Indicator (MBTI), do not specifically address money personalities but can be useful when advising couples.

The Moneymax Money Personality Profile, developed by Kathleen Gurney, PhD, measures 13 personality traits that, which according to Dr. Gurney's research, shape how clients make financial decisions. The traits measured are involvement, pride, emotionality, altruism, risk taking, confidence, power, work ethic, contentment, self-determination, spending, reflectivity, and trust. Using cluster analysis, these traits identify nine different personality types. The Moneymax Money Personality types are Entrepreneurs, Safety Players, Hunters, Optimists, Perfectionists, Achievers, High Rollers, Producers, and Money Masters. For a detailed description of each type, refer to the company's website at http://www.financialpsychology.com. Each money personality has its pros and cons when it comes to investing and accumulating wealth, with the Money Master being viewed as the ideal in this model. A Money Master has developed a healthy balance between self-confidence, risk taking, and trust in others and sees money as a tool.

Financial DNA, developed by Hugh Massie, is different from the Moneymax Money Personality Profile, as it measures both innate financial decision-making and risk-taking behaviors and shifts in money attitudes over time. According to Massie, "You have a unique Financial DNA code that originated and started evolving from the day of inception. Your Financial DNA will impact every financial, business, work, and life decision that you make."[4] The report produced discusses a client's financial DNA strands relative to 18 markers. These strands are need for control, information, decision making, advice receptivity, confidence, knowledge, education, expected results given core personality, goals orientation, advisor relationship, values, communication, management, risk, motivation, loss reaction, asset preferences, and investment preferences. The test taker is giving a low, medium, or high score relative to each strand. Financial DNA as a company also offers a situational DNA profile that should be tested annually, as it changes over time in response to life circumstances, a Communication DNA measure, and other measures. For more details, refer to the company's website at http://www.financialdna.com. The reporting of the Financial DNA test series is more complex and yields more data than the Moneymax Money Personality Profile, but it may overwhelm clients who prefer less detail. The Moneymax Money Personality Profile is fairly simple and easy to complete.

The MBTI is a personality test based on the theories of Carl Jung about perception and judgment. Katharine Cook Briggs and her daughter Isabel Briggs Myers further developed Jung's concepts and created the MBTI. This instrument contains four separate indexes, with each one reflecting one of four basic preferences. The preferences affect what people pay attention to and how they draw conclusions about what they perceive. The indexes are Extrovert-Introvert (E-I), Sensing-Intuition (S-I), Thinking-Feeling (T-F), and Judgment-Perception (J-P). The E-I scale measures how much a person draws energy from the outside world around him or her versus the inner world inside. The S-I scale shows how a person processes information, either through their senses or through intuition. The T-F scale indicates the type of judgment, rational or emotional, that a person is likely to trust when making a decision. The J-P scale describes whether a person prefers a structured lifestyle (judging) or has a spontaneous attitude (perceiving). Once the test is taken, clients are assigned a four-letter code, called a *type*. There are a total of 16 personality types, which are considered to have unique behavioral patterns and strengths and vulnerabilities.

For more details about the MBTI and personality types, refer to the Center for Applications of Psychological Type at http://www .capt.org.[5]

In his article "The Use of Typology in Financial Planning," Robert P. Hanlon, Jr., CFP, MSFS, discusses the value of using the MBTI in the financial advising process.[6] He proposes that advisors focus on two basic categories of preferences: Thinking and Judging types and Feeling and Perceiving types. Because Thinking and Judging types tend to be analytical and organized, they are often more open to picking investments using research and strategic planning. The Feeling and Perceiving types tend to be more heartfelt and prefer financial planning based on their values and beliefs. As you might suspect, there are a fair amount of couples who have a mix of these two types, making balancing their needs in a meeting challenging. However, if you understand that their style of communication and decision making is a function of how they perceive the world, it can be helpful. Also these types can be used to discuss similarities and differences in a couples approach to money and provide validation for their different, yet often complementary, skills in navigating the world.

IN HER OWN WORDS

I am a hopeless "P" (Perceiver). I have four knitting projects going, and I am reading three books. Unfortunately, my husband is a "P" too, so we really struggle to be organized and to get projects done before we start something else. It's like, oh, we haven't planned for our retirement, I don't have that life insurance policy purchased the way we said we would.

—*DIANA, 58-YEAR-OLD MARRIED BUSINESS OWNER, MOTHER OF TWO AND GRANDMOTHER OF THREE*

A study conducted by Jennifer Selby Long in 2007 titled "Are You a Wealthy Type?" concluded that Judging types, typically more plan-oriented individuals, are more interested in managing their finances, are more savvy about money managing, and receive more joy from managing their finances, regardless of gender. She also found that Perceiving types, especially women, did not do well in managing money. Her study concluded that 32 percent of Perceiving-type women ignored their finances, 44 percent lived in financial denial, and 41 percent were overwhelmed by their lack of financial literacy. Not surprisingly, these women were found to have the lowest incomes and net worth and reported being bored with or not involved in their financial lives. There were not enough Perceiving-type men in the study group for Long to draw any valid conclusions relative to men.[7]

Although the MBTI is a useful tool, it is complex and takes time and training to be able to administer. If this tool intrigues you, I recommend partnering with an MBTI Master Practitioner who can administer the test and interpret it for you and your clients. Refer to the MBTI Master Practitioner Referral Network at http:// www.mbtireferralnetwork.org for a list of consultants in your geo-graphic area. This will save you time and money and also show your clients that you care enough about them to collaborate with a pro-fessional who can provide this type of expertise to the team.

Another test that has proven useful in advising couples is the Kolbe A Index. The index was created by Kathy Kolbe and is a 36-question test that measures conative processing. Conative think-ing is defined as an action derived from instinct. According to this theory, every client has an equal capacity to be productive, but achieves it by drawing on different strengths. The Kolbe does not measure personality or IQ, but looks at how clients take action. The Kolbe assigns a score from "1" to "10" on each of four action modes: Fact Finder, how you gather and share information; Follow Thru, how you arrange and design information; Quick Start, how you deal with risk and uncertainty; and Implementor, how you handle space and intangibles. A high score in any mode indicates that you initiate solutions using this behavior and thrive in this area. A low score in any mode indicates that you prevent problems by using this behavior and find this a source of stress. Kolbe states, "Research indicates no significant differences in these patterns by age, race, gender, or physical handicap."[8]

According to Bill and Paula Harris, principals of WH Cornerstone Investments in Duxbury, Massachusetts, the Kolbe A Index is a useful tool for advising couples. Paula offered this example of the Follow Thru mode of action score: "If a client scores high in that area, we know they're going to follow up with us; everything's going to be organized; they're going to get back to us. If they prevent (score low) in it, then we know we are going to have to follow up with them more often." The Harrises shared an instance where the Kolbe was helpful. They learned that the husband of a couple they were working with was struggling to pay attention at every meeting. Once they had the clients complete the Kolbe A Index, they decided to restructure the couples meetings based on his scores. They gave the husband a quick summary at the beginning of the meeting because he prevented in the Fact Find area, which indicated that he just wanted the bottom line. They decided to meet with the wife for a longer period of time, as she needed more detail. Once they validated the husband's natural mode of operation and he was given permission to leave the meeting, interestingly, he became more engaged and decided to stay for the entire conversation.

Because Bill and Paula are a married couple who create financial strategies for clients who are couples, they decided to take the Kolbe themselves. Since that time, they have used this information in their personal and professional lives. Paula shared, "I'm very high in Fact Find, so I prefer a lot of information to make a decision. Bill prevents in Fact Find, which means he can summarize a situation very quickly and doesn't need as much detail to make the decision." Bill went on to say, "It's a great marriage tool. . . . I'm high in Quick Start. I'll come home on a Friday and say, 'Let's fly to France for the weekend,' and she'll be like, 'Oh my, I haven't researched France!'"[9]

IN HER OWN WORDS

The Kolbe really helped my husband and me see how our information needs and styles differ from one another in terms of financial planning. I saw that I was a Quick Start that requires relatively little information once I make a decision. My husband is more deliberative and enjoys seeing more information and research behind the investment recommendations. The Kolbe really helped us understand our intuitive styles and work better with our advisors.

—*SUE, 51-YEAR-OLD MARRIED MARKETING DIRECTOR AND MOTHER OF TWO*

The advantage to the Kolbe A Index over the MBTI is that it is easy to administer and relatively inexpensive. A client can go to the website, pay a modest fee, and take the assessment. Included is a downloadable report with an audio narrative by Kathy Kolbe detailing the person's individualized results. The other nice part of this test is that it emphasizes how all modes of operation come with strengths and challenges. This can be validating for couples who are stuck fighting about the *right* way to approach finances. By taking the Kolbe A Index and seeing their different modes of operation not as right or wrong, but as behaviors on a continuum, the couple can begin the process of accepting their differences and seeing the strength each brings to the advising process.

By understanding your clients and how they think, feel, and take action, you can set up a structure for couples meetings that works for their respective styles. As is true in most areas, clients value advisors who take the time to know them and learn how they prefer to communicate and operate in the world. Assessments such as the Moneymax Money Personality Profile, Financial DNA, MBTI, and the Kolbe A Index all help facilitate this process.

Money Styles

In addition to personality testing, there are also descriptive money personality styles that you can use with clients. These styles can be useful to share with couple clients to help them understand and appreciate their different approaches to money management and financial decision making. In the following paragraphs, three experts in the field of financial psychology describe money personality styles.

Joline Godfrey, author of *Raising Financially Fit Kids*, argues that children are born with money temperaments. She identified seven money styles: the hoarder, who always has a secret stash of money; the spendthrift, who loves to spend; the scrimper, who watches every penny and takes pleasure in saving; the giver, who loves to raise money for charity; the beggar, who has insatiable needs and constantly asks for more money; the hustler, who is a natural money negotiator and sees a deal in every transaction; and the oblivious, who refuses to focus on money at all. Godfrey encourages parents to look for these temperaments in their children and guide them in their financial literacy education accordingly.[10]

Olivia Mellan, author of several books, including *Money Harmony*, describes six major money personalities based on her work with individuals and couples. These include hoarders, spenders, money monks (clients who avoid having too much money), money avoiders, money amassers (clients who are most comfortable with large savings accounts), and money worriers. In her model, most clients are not one type but a combination of types. Mellan discusses how often opposite money personalities attract and how couples can use these descriptive styles to talk more openly about money and work through financial conflicts.[11]

Lastly, Deborah Price, author of *Money Magic*, describes eight money personality styles in her work.[12] Price's money personalities are based on archetypes she developed in her years working as a money coach. These styles are the innocent, who lives in denial about his financial life; the victim, who is prone to living in the past and blaming others for his financial situation; the warrior, who sets out to conquer the money world and is often good at investing and making money; the martyr, who is so busy taking care of others that he neglects his own financial needs; the fool, who plays by his own rules and is always looking for a financial windfall; the creator, who is on a spiritual or artistic path and has a love-hate relationship with money; the tyrant, who uses money to control other people; and the magician, who is wise, knowledgeable, and financially balanced. In Price's words, "The Magician is the ideal money type." What is unique about Price's work is that she believes clients have a primary money type and a "money shadow" type that is repressed. Her theory, based on Jungian psychological theory, states that clients need to become aware of their behaviors relative to money and learn to take on roles that are healthier given a particular circumstance. For example, if a client takes on a victim money style, she blames others for her poor financial situation. However, if she can learn to tap into the warrior side of her money style, she can learn to fight for what is rightfully hers and make more money. Either way, Price's approach empowers clients to be more aware of their attitudes toward money and more conscious in their financial lives.

As you can see, there is tremendous overlap among all these money styles. An "oblivious money type" in Godfrey's model could easily equate to a "money avoider" in Mellan's model and an "innocent" in Price's model. When selecting a model or theory to use with your couple clients, select the one that resonates with you and the type of clients you serve. For some, the simplicity of Mellan's work is enough; for others, the complexity and depth of Price's model is preferred. Having names that let you identify and talk about money styles between partners is helpful in assisting couples in understanding objectively that people think, feel, and act in varied ways relative to money. There is nothing *wrong* with their partners; they just think differently.

Overall, assessments and tools related to identifying clients' money personalities and styles provide clients and advisors with terms to use to describe thoughts and behaviors around money. Testing can be a fun way to educate couples about their money mindsets and is especially helpful if the couple needs some data outside their own experience to talk calmly and more rationally about money. Descriptive money styles also help normalize a client's experience, as they help clients realize that they are not alone in how they think and act toward money. Simply asking clients about their respective money mindsets in the first few meetings can be very useful.

No matter what tool you use, you are demonstrating to your clients that you care about more than just their assets. You are also concerned with how they think and feel about money, and you want to develop a financial plan and investment recommendations that tie into their personal values system. With female clients, this is especially useful in creating a trusting advisor–client relationship, as they often view money as a means to an end in taking care of their family. Whether you use testing or curious questioning to drill down into your couple's money mindset, it is an important part of the engagement and lays a wonderfully rich foundation for a good working relationship for years to come.

Summary

When you are advising couples, each individual in the partnership comes to the table with his or her own money mindset. As you have learned, clients are usually unaware of these money scripts that make up their money mindsets and often are at a loss to understand why they have different opinions about how to spend, save, gift, and invest. By teaching couples about money mindsets and what contributes to their thoughts and feelings about money, you can help them have more productive financial conversations. Together, they can decide which financial beliefs to use to make decisions and which ones to leave behind. With time and practice, their financial disagreements can be solved by uncovering the real root of the problem—different money scripts. Simply by taking the time to include the human side of finance in the advising relationship, you are proving that you are a couple-friendly advisor and one who provides great value to your clients.

Your Next Step: The Advisor's Money Mindset

It is important for you as a couple-friendly advisor to understand your money mindset before helping clients understand theirs. This mindset impacts how you react to your clients' thoughts and beliefs about money, the type of financial recommendations you make, and the financial success of your practice. Below are two activities to help you tap into your money mindset. First, complete these coaching exercises yourself, and then try them out with your clients.

Exercise I: Tapping Into Your Money Mindset
Take 5 to 10 minutes now to complete the following sentences. Complete this activity quickly, and do not edit your initial responses. Remember, there are no right or wrong responses, just the ones that resonate with you.

1. Wealthy people are _____

2. Poor people are _____

3. What my mother taught me about money was _____

4. What my father taught me about money was _____

5. My first money memory is _____

6. Asking people for money is _____

7. Talking about money is_____

8. The relationship between love and money is _____

_____

9. The relationship between spirituality or religion and money is _____ _____

10. People who pay retail prices are _____

11. People who will only buy items on sale are _____

12. Financial freedom means _____

13. Retirement means _____

14. The biggest financial lesson I want to teach my children or young people in my life is _____ _____

15. My current relationship with money can be described as _____

16. My partner's current relationship with money can be described as _____ _____

17. When I pay bills, I _____

18. When I save money, I _____

19. When I invest money, I _____

20. The biggest lie I tell myself about money is _____ _____

Now review your answers. Do you notice any themes in your responses? Where do you think these money scripts came from? How does each money script help you? How does each one potentially get in the way of your financial health? By identifying and examining your money mindset, you are better prepared to help your client couples with this type of exploration.

Exercise II: Turn Up the Volume

The human brain has a wonderful ability to focus on a particular item once you tell it to do so. This brain function is called the *reticular activating system*, and it can be used to help you turn up the volume on your money scripts. By noticing your money messages daily, you can collect useful data to help you understand your thoughts and beliefs about money and help your couple clients do the same.

Over the next week, jot down your thoughts and feelings in a small notebook or in your smartphone any time you engage in any money-related activity. At the end of the week, review your notes. Notice any trends in your thought patterns and highlight your most prominent money scripts.

Here is an example of a partially completed money script notebook:

MONDAY:

Bought new outfit for work; felt guilty and anxious as I paid for it.
"It was not on sale; therefore, I paid too much."

Deposited money into my Roth IRA; felt great and proud.
"Wise people save money for retirement."

Paid monthly bills while watching TV; anxious and distracted.
"Paying bills is painful."

TUESDAY:

New catalog came in the mail. Wish I could buy more clothes for work. Fear and sadness.
"Can't spend any more money on myself."

Car making a noise on the way to work. Dread. Fear. Anger.
"I can't afford a new car."

Husband and I discussed idea of getting a new car. Fought.
"Couples always fight about big purchases."

Prominent money scripts:
Guilt over spending money.
Saving money is a noble thing to do.
Couples always fight about money.
People who are wise save.

Noticing your money scripts on a regular basis helps you turn up the volume and bring these thoughts and beliefs into your conscious thought. The more you tap into your money scripts, the more skilled you become in identifying how these scripts impact your work with couples and your own financial health and well-being.

---------------------------(9)---------------------------

Manage Conflict

All married couples should learn the art of battle as
they should learn the art of making love.

—Ann Landers, syndicated advice columnist

ONE OF AMERICA'S GREAT PASTIMES IS WATCHING FOOTBALL. Two
opposing teams get on the field and fight it out to see who is vic-
torious. The goal is to get the "W" (win) no matter what it costs.
On a good day, the two teams on the field smack each other down
repetitively to get the pigskin to the end zone so that they can score
more points. On a bad day, players are carried off the field with broken bones and concussions before someone can claim victory. It is a
modern-day version of gladiators, with the fanfare, the intensity, and
the idea that the person who fights the hardest and is left standing at
the end of the game gets to live for another day.

What do you think football teaches clients about conflict? To
start, there is a winner and a loser. The conflict itself is messy, mean,
and sometimes bloody. The winner is admired, and the loser is pit-
ied. There are some rules of engagement, but they can be challenged,
and compromise has no place on the field. In football, engaging in
battle this way is part of the sport. But when you step off the field
into real life, conflict is a whole other ball game.

The problem is, some of your client couples may approach financial disagreements similarly to the way they would fight it out on the football field. They focus on winning, being the partner who is "right," and beating their spouse down until he or she throws in the towel. The outcome is about domination and power, not understanding and compromise. Now don't get me wrong. These clients can be lovely, intelligent, and a pleasure to work with until a disagreement arises. Then you see the gladiator inside emerge for a full-on attack, and you wonder, "What am I doing here?" Based on your history around managing and resolving conflicts, you want to either start yelling at the bully in the room or excuse yourself from the meeting and hide in the bathroom until they leave. While intellectually, you know you should hang in there and help them resolve their differences, you emotionally wonder how long the appointment will last.

Assisting couples in reconciling financial differences is an important service. It requires you to develop a certain skill set relative to conflict management, and it calls for you to confront your own thoughts and beliefs about money disagreements. There is such a thing as healthy conflict, and in this chapter, you will learn guidelines for facilitating productive financial conversations. In addition, strategies for empowering your couple clients to move from conflict toward positive change are included. If you are an experienced couples advisor, you already may excel at helping clients in this way and find this information validating. If you are newer to these concepts, don't fret. Many of us were raised in homes that were well intended but did not provide good role models for accepting and resolving differences. Why? Because most of us grew up watching football!

Myths About Conflict

Similar to how there are myths about couples and money, there are also misconceptions about couples and conflict. The top three myths about conflict that derail most couples when they attempt to resolve money disputes are presented here.

Myth 1. Conflict is a game with a winner and a loser. Some people love a good fight. They enjoy passionately arguing their position on issues and the rush of adrenaline that comes with winning good debate. However, these same individuals might struggle with fighting fair financially and resolving money conflicts with their romantic partners. The reason is that conflict, at its core, is about understanding, appreciating, and tolerating differences. It is not about winning at all costs.

Myth 2. Conflict is bad and should be avoided. Conflict is a healthy and essential part of couplehood. It helps couples grow and evolve, financially as well as emotionally. It is not inherently bad, but it is often associated with bad or uncomfortable feelings. The reason many clients associate negative emotions with conflict is that they have not had an opportunity to engage in a healthy financial disagreement. Your clients may have witnessed their parents fighting loudly about money and fear that they will scream and yell too. Or your clients could have come from a conflict-avoidant family where disagreements were swept under the rug in hopes that they would stay there and eventually evaporate into thin air. Either way, the two people in front of you may not realize how important it is to air financial differences in a calm and safe manner.

Myth 3. Conflict skills are innate. If I had a dollar for every time a client said to me, "I am just not good at conflict," I would be very wealthy. The belief expressed by many of my clients is that some people are born good at fighting and others are not. This could not be further from the truth. In fact, those clients who claim that they are good at conflict often need to learn to listen more than they talk. Those who profess that they stink at it often need to risk speaking up just a little more. The truth is that engaging in a productive conflict, or what I call "fighting fair financially," is a learned skill. With practice, conflict may never be your favorite activity, but it will become less daunting and more helpful in your relationship with money and your partner than you think.

Do you buy into any of the top three myths about conflict? If so, you are not alone. Few people without some formal training in conflict management and resolution approach disagreements with a positive attitude. This fear of conflict is often a result of early family messages about conflict, money, and the acceptance of different viewpoints. Remember back to when you were 10 years old, and two people in your family were having a disagreement. How did you know these two people were not getting along? Were they silent and avoiding each other? Did they yell and scream? Did they talk behind each other's back trying to elicit support from other family members? Or did they do something else? How you answer these questions tell you something about how conflict was handled in your family of origin and how you might engage in it as an adult.

In my work, I find that couples fall into two camps. The first camp is one where fighting resembles all-out warfare. There is yelling, screaming, and sometimes name-calling. Each person in the disagreement does his or her best to be heard, often by raising the volume of his or her voice, and spends little time, if any, actually trying to find out what the other person is saying. When I think of this style of communicating, I think of the television show *Seinfeld* and the Costanza family. The parents, along with George, their adult son, would yell and scream to make their points. No one ever seemed to listen, and conflicts ended when one of the Costanzas ran out of energy and needed to stop screaming for a while.

The other type of couple is the conflict-avoidant type. This couple hardly ever raises their voices to each other and never talks openly and honestly about money differences. On the surface, they appear healthier than the outwardly fighting couple, but they are just better at being quieter while not resolving differences. This couple reminds me of the newly married couple from the British royal family. They have conflict like every other couple, but you will never hear them utter a word about it publicly. No one knows what goes on behind closed doors, but my guess is that there is a lot of stuff swept underneath those beautiful, expensive heirloom rugs.

So were you born into the Costanza clan or the British royal family? Or maybe your parents were hybrids, a mix between the two styles. Either way, your family messages about conflict and money do play a role in your work with couples. Take five minutes and complete the following five sentences to gain some quick insights into your thoughts and attitudes toward money disagreements.

1. Fighting about money is_____

2. My parents taught me that money disagreements are_____

_____

3. In my current relationship, money conflicts are_____

_____

4. When my couple clients don't see eye-to-eye financially, I feel

_____

5. If I were to be truthful with myself, I would admit that conflict
   is _____

Use your answers to start exploring your personal beliefs about conflict. While it may be tempting to point a finger at your parents for not teaching you how to fight fair financially, remember that in our culture, this is a lost art. Instead, use this data to help you improve your skills in advising couples who are facing financial differences. It may even be useful to share that you don't have it all figured out either, but together the three of you can certainly work toward improvement.

The Truth About Conflict

Mary Parker Follett, a pioneer management consultant from the 1900s, once said, "There are three ways of dealing with difference: domination, compromise, and integration. By domination only one side gets what it wants; by compromise neither side gets what it wants; by integration we find a way by which both sides may get what they wish."[1] Boy, was she right! The goal of any healthy conflict is to understand both perspectives and arrive at a compromise that integrates the best parts of each viewpoint. While this sounds simple, the process takes time, energy, and, when it comes to money, often a well-trained financial advisor like you to facilitate the discussion.

IN HER OWN WORDS

I think in my first marriage I learned I wasn't as mature as I thought I was. I got into my second marriage, and I really want it to work. I realized that you don't always see things the same way as your partner; you respond differently. You react in a different speed. It was an "aha" moment.

—MYRA, 58-*YEAR-OLD DIVORCED AND REMARRIED FINANCIAL*

SERVICES PROFESSIONAL

Conflict is necessary and healthy in a partnership. Whether a couple is married, living together, or simply dating, learning to master the art of conflict is vital to the longevity of the relationship. A prominent family and marriage researcher, John Gottman, and his colleagues at the University of Washington declared in 1994 that they could predict which couples would divorce with more than 90 percent accuracy.[2] They used scientific observation and mathematical analysis to identify what couple interactions contributed to being happy in a marriage versus what behaviors did not. What they discovered was that happily married couples handled conflict in a gentle and positive way. Those who divorced did not. Gottman named these destructive behavioral patterns the "Four Horsemen of the Apocalypse"; they are described in the following sections.

Criticism. Criticism is defined as a complaint or episode of blaming paired with an attack on a partner's personality or character. These statements often start with the words, "You always" or "You never." For example, a wife says, "You never listen to me" when she wants to talk about the children's college fund. Or a husband declares, "You are crazy when it comes to money."

Defensiveness. Defensiveness is a behavior that occurs when clients defend their innocence or avoid taking responsibility for a particular problem by engaging in a counterattack. Often this behavior is seen as cross-complaining or whining. For example, the husband responds to his wife's criticism with a statement such as, "How can I listen to you when all you ever do is hound me about money?" Or the wife responds to her husband by shouting, "You think I am crazy about money; you are insane!" Neither one of these responses moves the conversation forward in a productive way.

Contempt. When criticism boils and festers, it turns into hostility and disgust. Contempt often involves sarcasm, mocking, name-calling, and belligerence, and is sometimes accompanied by a gesture such as rolling one's eyes or making an angry face. For example, a wife rolls her eyes and replies sarcastically, "Yeah. And you really want to hear what I have to say about money."

Stonewalling. This behavior happens when the listener attempts to withdraw from the conversation but offers no verbal or physical cues that he or she is affected by what the other person is saying. Hence the phrase, "Talking to you is like talking to a stone wall." For example, the husband turns on his computer while his wife is in midsentence.

As you can see, couples can quickly go from complaining to defending, than spiral into contempt and stonewalling. Think Costanza conflict types. The original issue, how can we save more for the children's education, is lost and replaced with a dysfunctional dialogue about each other's personal flaws. At this rate, the children will be fully grown and living outside the home before these two resolve this conflict!

IN HIS OWN WORDS

My parents always fought about money and put us kids in the middle of these arguments. The result is I find it very difficult to talk about money with my wife, or with anyone for that matter.
—*BENJAMIN, 63-YEAR-OLD MARRIED ENTREPRENEUR AND FATHER OF TWO*

Can a couple who is engaging in these destructive patterns be helped? Yes, couples can learn to identify their unhealthy communication patterns and adopt healthier ones. The following sections outline a list of behaviors happily married couples engage in or learn to adopt with conflict management coaching.[3]

Softened start-up. When one member of the couple has a complaint, the person is able to start the conversation in a gentle way, thus making the other partner more willing to listen. The focus of the communication is on a specific behavior or incident and is not an attack on the person's global personality. For example, suppose the wife in the above scenario said something like this: "I am concerned about the children's educational fund. Is there a good time we can sit down together to discuss my concern?" By using "I" statements and checking in to find out a good time to talk about this specific issue, the dialogue is softened and is more likely to be well received by the husband.

Turning toward our partner. This refers to how couples react to a request by their partner for emotional connection. The choices include turning away and ignoring the request, turning against and reacting with anger or hostility, or turning toward your partner, showing that you are open to listening and engaging in the connection. If the husband were to turn toward his wife, he would respond by saying, "Okay. Let me just put my work away and let's talk." If he is not in a good place to discuss this issue, he could even say, "Okay. Can we meet later today to talk, as I am working on something right now?" Each response indicates, that he is willing to connect and engage with his wife.

Repairing the conversation. This dynamic happens when the members of the couple work to de-escalate negative feelings during a difficult conversation. This can be in the form of an apology, a smile, or a bit of humor that breaks the tension. For example, as she smiles at her husband, the wife says, "I know that this is not your favorite topic, but I appreciate your willingness to talk with me about it."

Accepting influence. Husbands and wives who are more willing to be influenced by their partners have happier marriages. For example, the husband could respond, "I know it is not my favorite topic and appreciate you helping me talk about it."

As Gottman's work proves, couples fight. The fight is not the issue; how couples engage in disagreements is what matters. Some couples learn to shift their habits and improve their communication styles; others stay stuck in a battle of wills. Your only responsibility is to show them that there is another way when it comes to conversations about money. It is up to the couple to work toward change.

Facilitating Money Conflicts

As a couple-friendly financial advisor, it is important to learn techniques for helping couples work through financial differences and engage in financial conversations more productively. Although you are not a marital counselor, nor should you be playing the role of marital and family counselor, coaching couples on engaging in effective money conversations is within your purview. This type of coaching is valuable to your clients, and it is also good for business. If you assist partners in understanding and clarifying their financial goals, values, and dreams for the future, you can design and implement a financial plan and investment strategy that is more likely to be successful in the long term.

The dilemma for you as a conflict facilitator is that more often than not, a client's decision to interact with a partner is made on the unconscious level. This means that most of your clients do not overtly choose to interact with their spouses in a certain way, but do so based on their upbringing and what feels familiar. How the couple talks or does not talk about money, how they manage or don't manage their finances, and who makes or doesn't make the investment decisions are often done by default based on what their parents did or did not do. If the two members of the couple grew up with similar values and divisions of labor, conflicts around these decisions are minimal. However, if they had diverse upbringings, then their ideas about who does what can clash. Some couples find a way to work through these differences and even embrace diversity in their relationships. Others do not.

IN HIS OWN WORDS

When I'm honest and open with my wife, and we talk about money, we are actually getting closer as opposed to further apart.

—MATT, 40-YEAR-OLD SOCIAL WORKER AND MARRIED FATHER OF TWO

There are several traits a good conflict facilitator embodies. These include being curious, open-minded, nurturing, feeling-focused, a good listener, impartial, committed, and team-oriented. These attributes spell out CONFLICT. These characteristics need to be embraced if you are to assist couples with financial fights. They are also traits that you should encourage your client couples to practice. Let's look at each trait in a little more detail in the following sections.

Curious

Curiosity is a great tool for tolerating clients' difficult feelings and mitigating financial conflicts. It helps you to be in the moment with your clients when the discussion taps into strong emotions, either for you or for the clients. It allows you to wonder out loud about each client's individual perspective and assist the couple in hearing each other's viewpoint. Curiosity allows you to ask thought-provoking questions and be satisfied with not knowing the answers. When you are truly wondering about something, it is almost impossible to be upset, defensive, or judgmental. Therefore, bringing a healthy dose of curiosity to any couples meeting where money differences are being discussed is a good thing.

Open-Minded

Although similar to curiosity, open-mindedness is more about a state of mind than being inquisitive. To be open-minded involves being receptive to ideas and practicing the Zen principle of *beginner's mind*. Each time you have a conversation with a client, you pretend it is your first—that is beginner's mind. You let go of being an expert and allow the clients to be the experts on themselves. You stay open to all possibilities and to learning new things. Spend time with a five-year-old child to be reminded of how to have beginner's mind. Young children view the world around them with wonder.

For advisors who are trained to fix problems and provide solutions, developing the skill of beginner's mind may take time. But notice when you want to offer a tidy solution, and fight the urge.

There will be time for problem solving later, once the couple has had a chance to hash out the issue. Besides, any solution you provide at the start of the conflict resolution process won't be as viable as one offered at the end. So take a chance and step into your child's or beginner's mind at the beginning of each meeting, and marvel at what you discover about your clients.

Nurturing

When couples engage in effective conflict, they must allow themselves to be vulnerable with each other and with you. Therefore, it is vital that as the facilitator, you take a nurturing stance. This means that you champion the individuals for taking the risk of sharing financial imperfections and sensitive feelings. It also means that you cheer them on when the road to compromise appears endless. Lastly, nurturing can mean holding up a mirror that reflects back how the couple's words and actions don't match up or might be perceived by one party. When done in a caring way, this can be an effective tool for moving the couple's conversation toward a resolution.

IN HIS OWN WORDS

I anticipate that just about everybody's got tension in their marriage or their relationship surrounding money. So let's find out what it is and talk about it in a way that may be a little bit more healthy than waiting until somebody gets really pissed off or starts yelling.

—TIM MAURER, FINANCIAL PLANNER AND COAUTHOR OF
THE ULTIMATE FINANCIAL PLAN

Feeling-Focused

Couples often get bogged down in the concrete details of a money fight and fail to identify and talk about the underlying feelings that fuel the conflict. As a facilitator, you need to notice and label the feelings both parties are experiencing and bring these emotions to the surface. Don't worry; this is not the same thing as being a psychotherapist. You don't need to understand or dig deep into why they feel the way they do, just point it out. For example, a couple is arguing about how much to put in their son's college fund. They may get stuck talking about the amount of money and what they can afford, but fail to look at how putting money away for their child's future education feels. For one partner, it may feel great. For the other, it may bring up feelings of loss, as this partner didn't get this type of parental financial support. Changing the dollar amount of the allocation is not going to resolve the situation. Instead, identifying the underlying feelings associated with this financial decision and assisting the couple in talking openly about these diverse emotions will.

Listener

Being a good listener is an important skill in all aspects of advising clients. It is also imperative when mediating a financial disagreement. Often when partners are caught in a debate, their ability to listen to the other person is diminished. Therefore, you need to be the ears for both partners. Reflect back what each person said. Check in to make sure you understand the essence of their messages. And when in doubt, ask clarifying questions to elicit more precise information. Eventually, couples will be able to use the techniques you modeled in their meetings to begin to listen more effectively to each other.

Impartial

One of the hardest parts of facilitating a money conflict is staying impartial. It is easy to slip into taking sides, believing one person is more justified in his position than the other or thinking one partner is being unreasonable. Fight these urges because they often result from your own money history and your experience with conflict in your own family. While these are important factors for you to bring to your own relationship, they do not have a place in your client meetings. It is okay, and even helpful, if you notice quietly to yourself when you are aligning with one partner over the other. But the real challenge is maintaining neutrality and staying the course. Trust me—your clients will find the best solution for themselves when given the space to do so.

Committed

As the couple's financial advisor, you need to be committed to the process of conflict resolution. This commitment demonstrates to the couple that it is worth hanging in there when the conversation gets heated or emotionally trying. It also shows them that you care and you believe they will get to the other side of this money conflict. While it may take more time than you would like, hanging in there with your couple clients builds loyalty and ultimately makes your financial recommendation more applicable and more successful.

Team-Oriented

When a couple is arguing about money, I often ask them, "Whose team are you on right now?" This allows them to stop and evaluate how their verbal and nonverbal language is either inviting the other person into the conversation or pushing her away. Being on the same team does not mean always agreeing. But it does translate into both members of the couple working toward a shared goal that will improve the couple's financial life now and into the future. As a facilitator, notice when the couple is not on the same team, and work as a threesome to figure out how to get back on track toward a shared solution.

IN HIS OWN WORDS

I encourage couples to practice the "no shame, no blame" rule. This means that what happened in the past is now valuable only to the degree that it influences our behavior going forward. In hindsight, who made the mistakes doesn't matter, so let's move forward.

—*CARL RICHARDS, AUTHOR OF* THE BEHAVIOR GAP

Now that you know the traits that are important for you to embody as a money-conflict facilitator, it is time to look at a five-step method for helping couples engage in more productive financial conversations, both inside and outside of your office.

Five Steps for Engaging in Healthy Financial Conversations

As a financial advisor working with couples, you are in a unique position to teach clients how to engage in healthy financial conversations. The following is a five-step method for coaching couples on talking about money.

Step 1: Establish Ground Rules

It is important to establish and review ground rules before any financial conversation. Review the following basic rules for fighting fair financially with your clients at the beginning of a meeting. Also ask your couple clients to add a rule or two of their own if this helps in having a more productive money dialogue.

Be respectful. It is important to treat the other person in the conversation with respect. Listen actively, do not interrupt, and refrain from using profanity or blaming language. Blaming language usually starts with the word *you* and then makes a sweeping generalization about the other person's behavior. For example, "You always spend too much money and blow our budget" or "You never care about my feelings."

Do not mind read. Jumping to conclusions and attempting to read the other person's mind can result in frustration and anger that is unproductive and often unfounded. Do yourself and your partner a favor and ask questions instead of mind reading.

Use "I" statements. Start the conversation with "I am concerned about X, Y, and Z," not "You did X, Y, and Z." It may feel like a subtle difference, but it will get both of you started off on the right foot.

Take a deep breath before you speak. Sometimes the best response is to sit quietly and take a deep breath before speaking. This physiologically relaxes your body and clears your mind, so you can be more open and calm when talking with your partner.

Practice curiosity. Pretend you are a scientist interviewing a subject for a research project. Ask thoughtful, clarifying questions to learn more about your partner's viewpoint. When you are truly curious, you learn more and you are too busy wondering to pick a fight.

Step 2: Give a Crash Course on Couples and Conflict
Educate your clients regarding different styles of conflict management and how these styles are learned from parents or significant caregivers growing up. Share with them the difference between the Costanza style of fighting and the royal family style of conflict. Have them pick which style they most identify with or have them describe their own.

Once conflict styles are identified and discussed, review Gottman's Four Horsemen of the Apocalypse with them. Ask if

---

IN HER OWN WORDS

As early as I can remember, my young and divorced parents were in a battle over money. They were constantly in the court-room for money owed. These relentless financial battles defined my perception of money at a very early age. To this day, I do everything in my power to not let it be the cause of conflict in my own life.

—JACI, 32-YEAR-OLD MARRIED FINANCIAL SERVICES
PROFESSIONAL AND MOTHER OF TWO

---

they notice any of these patterns in their own behavior. Notice that I did not say each other's behavior. The focus needs to stay on each individual changing him or herself, not the partner. While the couple may resist this type of refocusing because of old habits, it is your job to remind them as often as necessary. Next, reassure them that all couples fall into these communication traps from time to time, and that conflict management skills can be learned. This step allows couples to enter money discussions armed with some basic information about conflict and couples, and a healthy dose of optimism about the potential outcome.

Step 3: Teach Active Listening Skills

Teach couples how to actively listen to each other. Actively listening is an effective technique for reducing disagreements and increasing mutual understanding. Use the following coaching exercise to assist couples in practicing active listening. When the couple is new to active listening, select a topic to discuss that is not emotionally laden. They need to build their listening skills and experience some success before they are ready to dive into deeper, more complex issues.

Start the conversation by having Partner 1 answer the following question, "What are you most proud of financially?" Partner 2 actively listens to Partner 1's answer. When Partner 1 is done answering the question completely, Partner 2 reflects back what he or she heard, starting with the following words: "What I hear you saying is . . ." It is vital that Partner 2 stick to the facts and, when possible, use Partner 1's exact words. If your clients insert judgments on what was said, gently ask them to reframe this behavior. Remind them that they will have time later in the process to express their opinions, but not right now.

When Partner 1 feels that Partner 2 has heard the message being communicated, it is time to switch roles. Now Partner 2 asks the question, "What are you most proud of financially?" and Partner 1 answers the inquiry. During this process, your role is to help the couple stay on track and not revert back to unhealthy communication patterns. It is likely that they will, especially in the beginning. Simply notice this out loud and redirect them when some adjustments to the communication are warranted.

Active communication takes time to master, so encourage your clients to practice this skill at home.

Step 4: Embracing Differences

The goal of any financial discussion is to find common ground where it exists, but not necessarily to agree on every point. Often the content that each partner is expressing is different, but the underlying values are the same. When this is the case, make this observation out loud. When different opinions emerge, remind clients that this is normal and natural. Differences are to be expected, so embrace them and agree to disagree as part of the process. Bring some levity to the conversation and have them think about marrying their mirror image. Often couples want this until they realize what would be lost if they were indeed identical money personalities.

Step 5: Celebrate Progress

"Progress, not perfection" is the old saying. This is definitely true when coaching clients on engaging in healthy money conversations. Encourage couples to celebrate each time they have a money conversation or work through a conflict. Not only does this reinforce that money conversations don't have to be miserable, down-and-out fights, but it reminds the couple that they are a team working toward a common goal. This is where football players can teach us a thing or two about conflict. Every time the team scores a touchdown, they celebrate.

Summary

One of the trickiest parts of advising couples is helping them identify and resolve money disagreements. Because many couples were brought up without good role models for conflict resolution, your job involves teaching them the myths about conflict and coaching them to develop the skills needed to engage in productive money conversations. To be most effective, examine your own attitudes and feelings about conflict and understand how this mindset may influence your ability to facilitate conversations about financial differences between couples. In the end, you and your clients will be better equipped to identify, manage, and resolve money differences as they arise inside and outside of your office.

Your Next Step: Visit Your Partner's Money Island

A great tool for examining diverse money beliefs and working through money conflicts is to have your couple clients visit each other's "money island."[4] Partners first identify their own money scripts, and then invite invite each other to visit their unique money island, complete with its customs and traditions. As with any visit to a foreign country, the objective of your visit is not to change the culture or to teach the residents how to adopt your money practices, but to learn as much as you can about the culture during your stay. Try this activity yourself first. You can do this with your romantic partner, a colleague, or a trusted coach. Then, once you understand the concept, invite your clients to go for a trip. Here are the steps to follow.

Step 1: If you have not done so already, complete the money questionnaire at the end of Chapter 8, "Uncover Money Mindsets." This helps you tap into the money scripts that make up your money mindset. Have your partner complete this exercise separately.

Step 2: Decide who is going to go on a money vacation first. To be completely objective, draw straws or flip a coin to decide the order.

Step 3: The first vacationer spends 10 to 15 minutes on the other person's money island. The resident gives a quick tour, explaining the money culture and the thoughts and beliefs of the islanders. The vacationer then asks open-ended questions to learn more about this place, but is not allowed to share his or her views with the residents. Once 10 to 15 minutes elapse, the vacationer spends 5 minutes putting together a scrapbook of the highlights from the trip. This is not shared immediately.

Step 4: The second vacationer now spends 10 to 15 minutes on the other person's money island. The procedure outlined in Step 3 is repeated.

Step 5: Now it is time for the two tourists to share their experiences with each other. Use the scrapbooks as a tool for facilitating the discussion. Talk about what you admired about the foreign land, indicate what things you found interesting, and share one or two money scripts that you want to borrow from the other partner's money island for the next week.

Step 6: After one week is over, spend a few minutes talking about what it was like to try on a different money script or two from your respective trips. Focus on the positive, and remember, as any good tourist would, to remain respectful of your host country residents.

The ultimate goal of this exercise is for couples to discover a new money land, called "Our Money Island," which is a blend of both worlds created from what each partner admired and liked from the other's individual money island. Although this activity takes some time, it is a fun way to start getting couples to see their differences from a more favorable vantage point. For clients who are kinesthetic learners, encourage them to physically move to another chair or corner of the room when they are visiting each other's respective islands. While this can feel a little hokey at first, the results will make you a believer.

10

Facilitate Lasting Change

> Consider how hard it is to change yourself and
> you'll understand what little chance you have
> in trying to change others.
>
> —William Shakespeare, English poet and playwright

HAVE YOU EVER WANTED TO CHANGE A HABIT BUT FOUND IT INCREDIBLY hard to accomplish? If so, then welcome to the human race. Change is hard for most of us, and often it takes several attempts before we are successful. Why? If you listen to diet and exercise commercials, you might believe you don't lose weight or tone up because you are lazy, weak, and unmotivated. But the real story is, change takes time. You may want to change but find yourself at a stage where you are doing it for someone else or you are still benefiting from staying the same. In my work with individuals and couples, I have helped many clients make lasting behavioral changes. But unlike the magic wand solution promised by the diet and weight-loss advertisers, it took time, small steps, and support to make it happen.

I often refer clients to the 1991 movie *What About Bob?* starring Richard Dreyfuss as a psychiatrist who goes on vacation to New Hampshire and Bill Murray as his neurotic patient who follows him. Bill Murray's character is told by the psychiatrist to take baby steps to conquer his fears. What unfolds is a comedy in which the doctor looks more unhinged by the minute as the patient begins to look saner. The poignant lesson in this film is that you need to take small, doable steps in order to change any behavior. The same is true with financial habits. Our tendency is to want things to change overnight. We take huge action steps that ultimately freak us out, and then we revert to what is comfortable. But when we slow down and take one tiny step every day—or every week—outside our comfort zone, we end up where we want to be.

As an advisor, you help clients every day identify spending and saving habits that are undermining their financial success. Often advisors are skilled at labeling these unwanted money habits but less equipped to assist clients in actually altering these behaviors. You may become impatient and not want to do this type of coaching. Or you may want to help but find the process difficult. In this chapter, you will learn why developing new financial habits or letting go of unhealthy ones is complicated and how you can work with both the individual partners and the couple to achieve lasting behavioral change. Let's look at how individuals and couples change financial habits in general.

The Stages of Change

In the late 1970s and early 1980s, two researchers at the University of Rhode Island, James Prochaska and Carlo DiClemente, conducted in-depth studies of how people change habits and eventually developed the Transtheoretical Model, also referred to as the Stages of Change Model, which is depicted in Figure 10.1. Their model was developed by examining how smokers gave up their cigarettes; however, the tenets of this theory are useful in understanding and assisting clients with financial change as well. The model highlights five distinct steps to modifying behavior. These are precontemplation, contemplation, preparation, action, and maintenance.[1] Each stage and how it applies to clients who are changing their relationship with money are described in the following sections.

Figure 10.1

Stages of Change Model

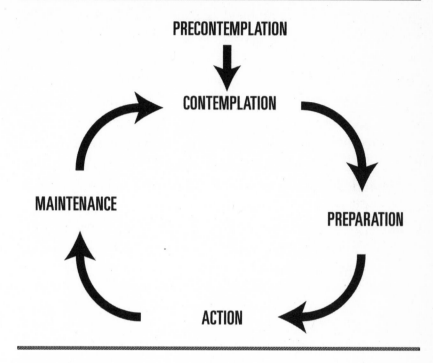

Precontemplation

Clients who are in the precontemplation stage are aware of the need to change but are not motivated to do so. Often they are being pressured by significant others to change their financial behaviors or are forced to examine their financial situation as a result of an event such as a death in the family, the birth of a child, or the sale of a business. They may say to themselves, "I should settle my dad's estate" or "My wife and I should have a retirement plan," but they have conflicting beliefs, such as "Settling the estate will be complicated and depressing" or "I'm too young to worry about retirement." Individuals in the precontemplation phase defend the status quo and are not ready to make any substantial and lasting changes.

Contemplation

The contemplation stage of change is marked by ambivalent feelings. Clients in this phase see their financial ways as unhealthy, realize that they have a problem, and may even hire you thinking that they are ready to take action. What they do not realize—and therefore cannot tell you—is that they have strong feelings about altering their spending, saving, and investing habits, and equally strong feelings about not altering them. For example, a couple says they want to save more money, but their spending habits continue to be excessive. Therefore, their savings account balance remains unchanged. Intellectually, the clients want to increase their savings, but emotionally, they continue to spend at the same rate because this habit is familiar and comfortable. Taking action is hard in the short run, so couples continue to think about making change in the long run, but fail to make any concrete shifts in their day-to-day habits to achieve their goal.

Preparation

Preparation is marked by a clear commitment to change. In addition to working with you, clients at this stage may be reading financial books, magazines, or blogs; talking to friends about investing; taking financial literacy workshops; or actively engaging in planning discussions. Also known as the "determination stage," this phase is marked by questions such as, "What action can we take now to better manage our money?" and statements such as, "We are determined to fully fund out retirement accounts" and "Tell us what to do, and we will do it."

Action

Most clients (and advisors, for that matter) want to be in the action stage. This stage involves taking steps such as debt reduction, budgeting, and conscious financial planning. These action steps reinforce the couple's belief in their ability to make positive progress. However, clients need to work through the other stages of change previously outlined to truly be ready for the type of meaningful action that occurs at this stage. Research shows that clients spend less time in the action phase than in any other. Estimates range from as little as one hour to as long as six months. It is human behavior to then either circle back to a previous stage or move forward into maintaining the new habit.

Maintenance

After couples have altered their money habits, integration of their new behaviors is the primary goal. It is important for clients to avoid temptations and be aware of triggers that can cause them to revert to their old behaviors. At this stage, clients should anticipate problematic money situations and think about how to handle them differently from in the past. Old money messages may pop up again. It is imperative to reinforce good investment practices and remind the partners of their progress at this stage.

IN HIS OWN WORDS

Developing a new habit or practice is hard for me. At first I put a rubber band around my wrist to remind me that I am committed to doing something new. Eventually, I don't need the visual cue.
—JAY, 55-YEAR-OLD DIVORCED AND REMARRIED SALESMAN

Changing financial behaviors can be a slippery slope. Relapse happens, and couples may slip back into old unhealthy behaviors. Don't fret, as this is part of the process. When a couple slips, do not throw in the towel. Instead, notice this slide backward in your next meeting, and help the partners examine what triggered the fall back into unhealthy habits. Focus on what they can learn from this experience, and assure them that a slip in a behavior does not mean a full relapse. It just means that it is time for a tune-up. Take this opportunity to show your value as their financial advisor by guiding them through a series of questions to help them identify the triggers that contributed to the slip. Then offer them strategies to assist them in returning to where they were before the relapse. Only through learning from money mistakes can clients and couples cope differently going forward.

Remember, a slip does not have to be a complete slide. True relapse happens only when you put the blinders on, stick your head in the sand, and become unconscious. So help your clients stay mindful of what they are trying to accomplish.

Couple Dynamics and Change

The Stages of Change Model is helpful when coaching clients on an individual basis. However, when advising couples, there is one more factor to consider. This is the effect of the couple dynamic on the change process. As mentioned in Chapter 3, "Advising and Couple Dynamics," partners crave balance. Therefore, when one person attempts to alter a financial habit, the other person is also required to change. Often this is when trouble ensues because, together, they unconsciously collude to stay the same.

For example, say Tom decides in an advising meeting that he needs to meet weekly with his partner, Jeffrey, to help him stay on track with the budget they created with you. Tom indicates that this meeting will help him be more conscious about his spending, and his partner, the one who has his spending under control, agrees. The first week, both make time for the meeting, and the strategy is effective. The second week, Tom declares, "I would rather read my book." Jeffrey is annoyed but picks up a book and starts reading too. Together they have let each other off the hook and maintained the status quo. To move toward the change Tom says he wants, he will have to make this meeting a priority, and Jeffrey will have to hold him to this commitment. To avoid conflict (which inevitably comes with change), neither partner addresses the issue. So the original balance in the relationship is maintained.

This is a wonderful example of how couples "dance" together, and how when one individual decides to do something new, the other may engage in a change back behavior. Let's take a minute to explore how this occurs.

The Dance

All couples engage in a dance that is unique to them. This dance involves how they communicate, interact, and negotiate. It also includes how they manage money. If one person decides to change his or her financial dance, then the other person, by default, needs to learn new dance steps. What is interesting about this phenomenon is that one member of the couple will say that he wants his partner to change; however, when the partner does so, he unconsciously sabotages the effort. This is what is called a *change back* behavior in psychology.

Here is a common example. A wife wants her husband to be more actively involved in their financial life, so she requests that he pay bills with her. At the first joint bill paying session, the wife discovers that this task now takes longer and that her husband wants to negotiate which bills get paid first. In the past, she had complete control over this process. With him participating, she now feels second-guessed and frustrated. After their second bill paying session together, she tells her husband, "This is a waste of time. I will just do it myself." She resumes doing this task solo, but remains resentful of her husband for not pulling his weight. Her husband is relieved because his money script says, "I am no good with money," and he believes it's best for her to manage the family finances.

This common scenario is what happens when couples try to change their financial dance. They find it uncomfortable emotionally and realize that doing something new is initially time-consuming. This is where you come in and add value because couples need support, coaching, and accountability if they are not to engage in change back behaviors that undermine their efforts.

Change Back!

In her book *The Dance of Anger*, Harriet Lerner, PhD, introduces the concept of change back behaviors. She states that the minute a person alters a behavior, it is met with resistance both internally and externally. She writes, "This 'Change back!' reaction will come both from inside our own selves and from significant others around us. We will see how it is for those closest to us who often have the greatest investment in our staying the same, whatever criticism and complaints they may openly voice. We also resist the very changes we seek. This resistance to change, like the will to change, is a natural and universal aspect of all human systems."[2]

IN HIS OWN WORDS

I have to be more responsible with money now that I'm getting divorced. My ex-wife would always cover for me financially, so I didn't have to learn to be financially responsible. With the divorce, I need to learn how to cook, clean, and balance a checkbook.

—DON, 64-YEAR-OLD DIVORCED BUSINESS CONSULTANT AND FATHER OF THREE

In the preceding example of the wife and husband, it is clear that the wife wanted her husband to participate in bill paying but is resistant to the change that she seeks. Her husband is ambivalent about this new agreement and therefore bails on the new system the minute he is given the opportunity. This is where you can be helpful.

As a couple-friendly advisor, you can educate your clients regarding change back behaviors. By anticipating this as part of the change process, each partner can be on the lookout for this tendency in him- or herself and the significant other. Also you, as an objective outsider to the couple dynamic, can notice signs of these behaviors and help them stay the course until they learn some new dance steps and practice for a while.

The New Dance

In time, couples learn new steps to their partnership dance. With practice and patience, couples fall into a new rhythm, similar to yet different from their original one. Partners who spend a lifetime together grow and change together. Sometimes, one person takes the lead and the other follows. At other times, the roles are reversed. Over a couple's life span, this change process is replicated numerous times relative to the many facets of their lives. Finance is just one of them, but an important one.

Let's look at a case study that exemplifies how an individual moves through the stages of change and the impact of couplehood on the change process.

A Case Study: The World's Best Shopper

Tina and Matt are a wonderful illustration of how couples change, how the partnership shifts gradually over time, and how they need to work toward change together. I was fortunate enough to work with this couple and help them take the important and scary step of letting go of an unhealthy, but familiar financial dance. Initially Tina was identified as the "patient" by her husband, Matt. But as their story reveals, in time, they both discovered that they were an important part of the final solution. Let's look at how this unfolded.

When Tina started wealth coaching, she was one of the world's best shoppers. Always impeccably dressed, she loved fashion and spending money on clothes, shoes, and accessories. Her husband gave her an ultimatum the night before she called to make her first appointment. She did not think her shopping was a problem, but Matt did and had threatened to stop paying her credit card bills if she didn't end her habit. It was clear in our initial session that Tina was firmly planted in the precontemplation stage of change. The only reason she was sitting in my office talking about her financial habits was her husband's insistence that she get help.

Tina and I discussed her shopping routine, her history of buying clothes to feel less lonely, and how she binged on clothes just like she binged on food. I educated her about what it would take to stop her unhealthy behaviors, and how she would need to look at her feelings as well as her behaviors concerning money. At the end of our time together, Tina set up a follow-up coaching appointment, but a few days later canceled it. She was just not ready to change.

Three months after our initial meeting, Tina called me in tears. She said, "When I am sad, I shop. When I am angry, I shop. When I am bored, I shop. All I do in life is shop! Matt is so angry at me I think he is going to leave me this time for sure." I validated her strong feelings and invited her in to revisit the idea of working together. She agreed.

This time, Tina was more engaged in the process. She shared with me how she was anxious to let go of her numerous weekly trips to the mall and was afraid of what would happen to her marriage and her for financial situation if she did not. She was both grateful to Matt for financially supporting her and angry that she "had to be taken care of," as he so often put it. Tina was clearly on the fence about changing her behaviors and had moved into the contemplation stage of change. Together, we discussed that it was okay to receive coaching even if she was not 100 percent ready to make a change in her spending. She seemed relieved to know that I would not pressure her to stop spending, which was something she wished other people in her life would do.

Over the course of our work together, Tina examined her money scripts, her family money messages, and how she had learned to use shopping to cope with life's ups and downs. She learned how to slow down her knee-jerk reaction to emotional events of heading to the mall and replacing it with deep breathing, journal writing, and positive self-talk. By discovering new coping skills, Tina had moved into the preparation stage of change. She was setting the stage for letting go of her destructive shopping behavior once and for all.

Shortly after, Tina moved into the action stage of change. She shopped less compulsively and eventually replaced this destructive habit with healthier ones, such as journaling, calling a friend, or sharing her feelings with her husband. As she reduced her shopping behaviors, she verbalized more of her feelings to Matt, and this caused friction in her marriage. Matt believed that all she had to do was stay out of the mall and everything would be fine, but he discovered that his financial behaviors and attitudes also contributed to the problem.

As part of her work, I invited him in for a few sessions to discuss how, as a couple, they would need to operate differently financially. Eventually, Tina discovered that she wanted to return to work, even though she monetarily did not need to do so. Work gave her a sense of purpose and allowed her to feel some independence from her husband, which she discovered she needed. At first, Matt was reluctant to let her work, as he believed a good husband provides for his wife, and if she was working, somehow he was failing. We had identified his change back behaviors and how both partners would need to learn a new dance when it came to making and managing money in the house. Tina's shopping habit improved, as did the couple's marriage. The last time I met the couple, Tina was being more financially responsible and was happy at her new job. She beamed when she shared that "Matt and I are saving *together* for our dream vacation home." They were learning and practicing new steps.

All clients change financial habits in small baby steps. Identifying the stage of change that an individual or couple is in relative to a financial habit is empowering, both for you and for the couple. This awareness can lead to action, but first the partners have to pass through a series of predictable, yet important stages. As a couple-friendly advisor, educate your clients about this model and assist them in taking the sometimes anxiety-provoking steps necessary to move closer to financial health.

Summary

Change takes time. However, you can help couples take steps toward identifying what stage of change they are in and educate them as to how each member of the partnership needs to be part of the process. The Stages of Change Model is helpful for your clients because it provides insight into why developing new financial habits or letting go of unhealthy ones is challenging. It also assists you in appreciating the complexities and the amount of time required for couples to take meaningful action. The next time a couple says they want to alter their financial behaviors, sit back and watch their dance. Then gently coach them toward learning a few new moves.

Your Next Step: How Do You Change?

Take a minute and think about a time in your life when you changed a behavior. It does not need to be related to money. Maybe you quit smoking, started exercising, or stopped swearing. Now write down exactly how you changed this habit. Use the following seven questions as a guide.

1. What was your habit like before you wanted to change?
2. What triggered a desire to change?
3. Was it a person, place, or thing that moved you to let go of this unhealthy behavior and/or start a new one?
4. What was it like when you first started the process of change?

5. What made it difficult?

6. What parts of doing something new were easy or motivating?

7. How did you integrate this new behavior into your life in a lasting way?

By looking at how you changed your habits, you learn something about how people change in general. Use this exercise to guide your clients toward understanding how they change their habits and how you can support them as their trusted advisor along the way.

---11---

Empower Couples to Raise Financially Intelligent Children

Give a man a fish and you feed him for a day; teach a
man to fish and you feed him for a lifetime.

—Maimonides, medieval Jewish philosopher

BEING A PARENT IS NOT EASY. YOU WORRY ABOUT YOUR CHILDREN'S
safety, their economic future, and their ability to navigate an increasingly complex world. Boys and girls are bombarded with messages
about celebrity, money, and wealth before they are developmentally
equipped to process them. Reality shows focused on attaining fame
and fortune overnight with stars who spend money haphazardly on
luxury cars, electronic toys, and expensive nights on the town are
more in vogue than saving for college. Although the media usually
presents an image that is just out of reach of the masses, the gap is
widening every day. Even proactive parents who try to protect their
children from these mass media money messages find it hard to stop
the momentum. This leaves your couple clients looking for solutions
to help them raise financially savvy kids in an increasingly materialistic
and wealth-obsessed culture. As an advisor, you are uniquely equipped
to be a big part of the solution for parents in need of these services.

Parental Fear

According to Merrill Lynch's "World Wealth Report: 2011," 69 percent of high-net-worth individuals surveyed agree that the next generation is not adequately prepared to manage their inheritance.[1] Their fear is that their children will end up feeling entitled because of the family wealth and waste their lives partying into the wee hours of the night without any real sense of purpose. All you have to do is look at celebrities such as Paris Hilton, Lindsay Lohan, or the Kardashians for examples of the types of stories that keep these parents up at night. While the fear runs high in families with substantial wealth, it is also a concern for those of lesser means. In a society that celebrates celebrity over talent, I am sure you can see why.

Many parents who are concerned remain silent on this issue. Their hope is that not mentioning the family's wealth or not talking directly about money and wealth will make the problem go away. However, not proactively addressing these worries leaves the outcome up to fate. The old saying goes, "Silence is golden," but in this particular situation, it is dangerous. Studies have found that 70 percent of families fail to successfully transfer wealth to future generations primarily because of poor family communication about money and lack of preparation of the next generation.[2] With some coaching, families can learn to talk more openly about money and teach their children important financial lessons.

Couples need your guidance and expertise to assist them in rearing well-balanced children who are financially literate and, if the situation warrants, emotionally capable of inheriting wealth. In this chapter, you will learn tips for coaching parents on this issue, the common questions parents want answered, and how to work with couples to make sure their children grow into financially intelligent adults.

More than Money Management

Rearing financially thoughtful children involves more than just teaching young people about the mechanics of money. It involves teaching them to be financially intelligent. *Financial intelligence* is defined as having the financial knowledge, skills, and insight into your relationship with money to enable you to responsibly save, spend, invest, and pass on wealth. *Knowledge* includes understanding basic financial concepts, such as budgeting, saving, investing, and charitable giving. *Skills* refers to using this knowledge to perform basic financial tasks, such as balancing a checkbook, calculating compound interest, and reading and understanding financial documents. The last component, *financial insight*, is defined as having an understanding of the underlying thoughts, feelings, and attitudes that influence your financial behaviors. While some financial literacy programs leave out learning about money personalities and financial insight, this is actually an important component of financial intelligence. It is only when a person can understand how he or she makes financial decisions and the values being expressed through these habits that he or she can learn how to live at peace with money and wealth.

IN HIS OWN WORDS

My wife and I have always tried to instill a sense of financial knowledge into our two kids, with the intention of having them be financially responsible and independent. We did that by helping them understand how to save and spend gift and babysitting money; by assisting them to open bank accounts while in elementary school; and by encouraging and supporting them in finding summer and on-campus jobs while in college. We hope we've empowered them with a sense of financial literacy.

—*STEVE, 50-YEAR-OLD MARRIED DIGITAL MEDIA DIRECTOR AND FATHER OF TWO*

As mentioned in Chapter 8, "Uncover Money Mindsets," a person's money personality is typically formed between the ages of 5 and 14. This is the time when children and young adolescents are witnessing parents, grandparents, and other important caregivers manage money. By watching others talk, save, spend, and invest money, the young person develops a set of beliefs, called *money scripts*. These money scripts follow the young person into adulthood and influence his or her financial habits. If a solid foundation is laid, and a child understands how to identify money beliefs and attitudes in the decision-making process, unhealthy financial behaviors can be avoided later in life.

In addition to learning financial intelligence, a young person who is due to receive a substantial inheritance needs to develop a high level of emotional intelligence to be able to skillfully navigate the land of wealth. *Emotional intelligence* is defined as having an ability to identify and express feelings and understand how your words and actions impact those around you. An heir with high emotional intelligence is less likely to be burdened by wealth, less likely to be ripped off by unethical business and financial associates, and more likely to live a satisfying life. He or she has self-awareness, a sense of personal power in the world, and the resilience to bounce back from life's challenges (see Figure 11.1, Preparing the Next Generation).

Overall, coaching your clients to teach their children how to have a healthy relationship with money is a great value-added service. It draws on your existing expertise, and it shows your clients that you care about the well-being of the entire family. It also helps you determine your couple's current level of financial intelligence and identify and fill in any gaps in their basic money skills. With a little creativity, you and your couple clients can have fun, further solidify your role as a trusted advisor, and help prepare the next generation to receive wealth.

Three Truths About Financial Literacy

When it comes to teaching children about financial literacy, it is important to remember three simple truths. These are (1) start early, (2) capitalize on teachable moments, and (3) it is never too late to

Figure 11.1

Preparing the Next Generation

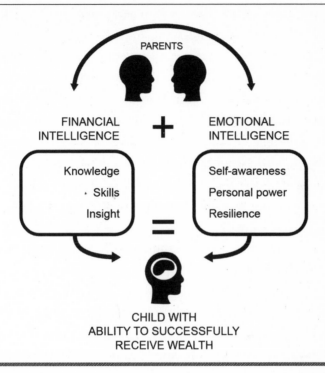

teach children about money. Each truth is listed below with a brief description. As you read these tips, think about how you can bring these elements into your practice with couples.

Start Early

All financial literacy experts agree that it is best to start talking with children about money at around five years of age. The reason for starting so young is that this is the age when a child begins to be aware of money and develops beliefs about it. Think back to the story I shared in Chapter 8, "Uncover Money Mindsets," about my shiny red toy cash register. I was five years old at the time, and it was my first impressionable money memory. Now take a minute to ponder your first money memory. How old were you? Chances are it was around this same age.

Financial literacy training needs to be age appropriate. Therefore, teaching a five-year-old child about interest rate risk, hedge funds, or the global economy does not make sense. Not only does a child this age not have the ability to think abstractly, which these concepts require, but these concepts are not applicable to his or her life. Instead, teach a young child the name of each coin and its corresponding monetary value. Have children practice making change, and start to introduce them to the concept of *wants* versus *needs*. Any trip to the store will present numerous opportunities for parents to help children figure out what they need versus what they wish they could have. This is also a good age to introduce them to the idea of philanthropy. For example, encourage parents to discuss with their children what they care about and why. Find a charity tied to this cause, and have the parents assist the child in making periodic donations. This can be as simple as putting a percentage of the child's monetary gifts into a special piggy bank for this reason.

Encourage parents to continue to teach money lessons consistently over time, and tie these activities to the young person's social and emotional development. Some concepts will be repeated over time, and some will be introduced along the way. For example, an eight-year-old boy who is interested in starting a dog-walking service in his neighborhood can learn how to set a price for his services, how to collect money from his customers, and the value of hard work. A 16-year-old boy starting a similar dog-walking service can also learn these important money skills; however, he may also be ready to tackle accepting credit card payments and using a financial software program to manage his cash flow.

A great resource for how to help your clients teach their children about money is the book written by Joline Godfrey titled *Raising Financially Fit Kids*. This book uses childhood developmental theory and 10 basic money skills to guide parents on how to raise financially literate children. The 10 basic money skills include the following:[3]

1. How to save
2. How to keep track of money
3. How to get paid what you are worth
4. How to spend wisely
5. How to talk about money
6. How to live on a budget
7. How to invest
8. How to exercise the entrepreneurial spirit
9. How to handle credit
10. How to use money to change the world

The book contains activities, discussion topics, and resources appropriate for different age groups for further exploration of each of these money skills. It is a great guidebook for advisors coaching parents on raising financially savvy children, and it makes a wonderful gift for those couples with young children.

Capitalize on Teachable Moments

To make teaching children about money manageable in the in busy lives, it is helpful to teach parents how to capitalize on teachable moments. *Teachable moments* are defined as opportunities for learning that come up during the course of a day. They are not planned or expected. A parent who has been coached to raise financially literate children can use these teachable moments to engage in conversations with his or her children about an important money lesson on an impromptu basis. Besides being easier to fit into a family's busy day, teachable moments are often more effective learning tools than a random lecture about saving and spending money from a concerned parent.

While teachable moments are, by their nature, unplanned, it is a good idea to help couples consider how daily activities can be easily turned into opportunities for learning. Here are a few ideas about how a parent might seize the moment.

A trip to the grocery store: This is a great place to teach young people about reading price labels, comparison shopping, and making a budget and sticking to it.

Picking up the mail: When a bill comes in the mail, open it with your child. Have him or her read it to you and ask questions. Start with bills that are easier to read; then, as the child masters this skill, review more complex statements. Advise parents to remain calm and relaxed during this exercise, as they don't want the child to connect negative feelings or stress with paying bills.

Shopping for gifts: Parents often complain about all the birthday parties their kids get invited to and the related expenses. Instead of complaining, turn this chore into a teachable moment. Discuss how much the family wants to spend on each friend's gift and establish a shopping budget. Take your child to the store and stick to this amount. Often this is a challenge for parents who want to please their children or avoid having their children make a scene. Support parents in setting and keeping the monetary limit, even if the child has trouble initially. Remind them that this is an easier and less expensive lesson at 7 than at 17 years of age.

Watching television: Television shows contain many messages about money and wealth. Encourage your clients to think about the television shows they enjoy as a family and the money messages embedded in each. The next time they watch one of these programs, encourage them to challenge their children to a contest to see who can discover the most money messages in the plot. Not only is this fun, but it is also a great way to start a discussion about finance without it being stuffy and dull.

Plan a family vacation: Another gripe some parents have is that kids don't appreciate how much they spend on vacations. If this is the case, then it is time for the parents to include the children in vacation planning. As you can imagine, when planning a vacation, there are many great opportunities to talk to kids about money. Start early and give each child an imaginary budget. Challenge the child to design a vacation within budget to a place he or she would like to visit. Make sure the children realize that the final decision is up to mom and dad, but that their proposals will be given serious consideration. If the children are too young to be planning an entire week, then give them a budget for one day of vacation instead. Either way, use this activity to talk about financial decision making, how to balance individual needs in the family, and the importance of spending within your means.

There are numerous teachable moments in the life of a family. Offer these ideas, and also brainstorm with your couple clients to create their own. Remember to make it fun and to focus on participatory learning; caution parents about turning these moments into lectures.

It's Never Too Late

When I interviewed female clients for my book *How to Give Financial Advice to Women*, I was surprised when some of my interviewees stated that it was too late to teach their children about money. Often their children were in their late teens or early twenties. It saddened

---

IN HER OWN WORDS

So many young people don't balance their checkbooks anymore. I have a 22-year-old niece who actually goes online to check her bank balance before she goes out with her friends so she knows how much she can spend!

—*DEBBIE, 45-YEAR-OLD MARRIED BUSINESS PROFESSIONAL AND AUNT* me to think how many parents give up on being financial mentors. I detected that most of these women felt a sense of disappointment for not having been more proactive about financial literacy when their children were younger. When I told them it was not too late, many just laughed. Others started to consider how they could broach the subject currently.

The truth is, it is never too late to teach your kids about money. In a perfect world, every parent would impart financial lessons to their children between the ages of 5 and 14, as the experts recommend. But life is flawed and complicated. Many parents do not have a road map on how to handle their own finances, let alone teach their children how to do it well. This is exactly why you need to coach parents on how to be good financial role models. You know finance better than most people do, and you can translate complex concepts into simple terms that parents can then pass on to the next generation. Remind parents that a good financial role model is not perfect, but makes mistakes and learns from them. Conversations about financial successes, failures, and life lessons are timely at any age. I have witnessed children in their forties and fifties learning new money messages from their parents. No matter what the age of the children, when parents take the risk of opening up about money, celebrate it as a victory, as it is truly never too late.

Now that you know these three truths, it is time to discover what types of questions parents have when it comes to raising financially intelligent children.

Frequently Asked Questions

Below are questions that parents routinely ask relative to the subject of raising financially savvy children. Some of the questions apply to younger children, and some to young adults. The answers provided are based on my expertise in the field of financial literacy and on conversations with financial advisors over the years. Feel free to use them as a guide when asked these questions in your office.

Question: *How can we teach our kids the value of saving money early in life?*

Answer: The easiest way to teach children how to save money is to give them a weekly allowance. Encourage your clients to start paying an allowance at around age 5 and make sure the dollar amount is appropriate to the child's age. Often $1 per year of age is a good measure. Stress to the parents that an allowance should be used as a teaching tool, not as reward or punishment for good or bad behavior. The goal of giving an allowance is to help children learn how to save for bigger purchases and also spend money from time to time for enjoyment. To aid in this process, instruct parents to have their children divide their weekly allowance into three buckets—one for saving, one for spending, and one for giving. Make this a fun project for the kids by having them make and decorate three piggy banks (mason jars are great for this project) and label them "savings," "spending," and "giving." Each time they put their money into the three buckets, they learn how to budget and that money is meant to be used in a variety of ways, as opposed to being spent the minute it is received.

Question: *Should we give our children an allowance, and if so, what is an appropriate amount given their ages?*

Answer: As mentioned earlier, an allowance is a great tool for teaching children how to manage money. If possible, start early, around age 5, and make the allowance a small amount, such as $5 for a 5-year-old, $12 for a 12-year-old, and so on. The idea is to give them enough to be able to save up for a treat at the end of the month, but not so much that they take the money for granted. It is important to increase the amount periodically and to be consistent in paying the allowance. If your clients have not started an allowance system early on, assure them that this is okay and that there is still time to teach important money lessons.

It is also helpful to ask your clients if they received an allowance when they were growing up, and, if so, how it was used by their parents. Talk with them about the money lessons they learned by having an allowance and what they would like to pass on to their children. This helps you gain some insight into their values and also helps them be more effective at financially empowering their children.

Question: *Should we pay our children for doing chores around the house?*

Answer: There are conflicting viewpoints from financial literacy experts on how to answer this question. The first group believes an allowance should not be tied to chores because children need to learn that, as family members, it is part of their job to help out around the house. The other camp believes it is okay to pay children for chores as long as these tasks are not part of their routine family responsibilities. For example, if a parent needs help raking the leaves, and this is above and beyond what is typically expected of their child, then offering to pay for this work may be appropriate. Or if the neighborhood is having a yard sale, and the young person wants to help the parents out by staffing their booth, giving her a

---

IN HIS OWN WORDS

Some parents like the idea of teaching financial responsibility early by rewarding their kids for work completed around the house. The kids are then allowed to spend some of the money earned as well as save and donate some of it. Then the kids have to make decisions about future purchases based upon their savings. It helps them learn about delayed gratification for really important things rather than impulse purchases. Also, the donate part teaches kids to think about others who may have needs greater than theirs.

—*BILL HARRIS, FINANCIAL PLANNER WITH WH CORNERSTONE INVESTMENTS*

percentage of the profits teaches her about being entrepreneurial. My recommendation is to talk with your client couples about these two different viewpoints and the pros and cons of each, and then let them decide, with your guidance, on the best answer for their family.

Question: *How do we teach our children that money doesn't magically come from an ATM machine?*

Answer: The first way is to use cash. It can be a great teaching tool for parents to occasionally use cash to pay for purchases such as groceries, gas, meals, movies, and so forth. Have the children count out the amount due for the purchase and then give it to the cashier. After the purchase, discuss what it is like to give money away and get only a few dollars back. From time to time, have the children do the same exercise, but this time paying with a credit or debit card (with parental support and signatures, of course). Ask them how it felt different to hand the cashier a plastic card rather than cash. Instead of telling the children, the parents are giving them an actual experience to draw upon that speaks to how easy it can be to just hand someone a plastic card.

In addition to the activity above, encourage your clients to talk openly with their children about their personal values and how they express them through spending and saving money. This conversation will be effective only if you practice what you preach, so make sure that the parents are exhibiting financial habits that are congruent with these values on a regular basis.

Question: *What should teenagers be expected to pay for with their own money?*

Answer: The answer to this question is that it depends on the couple's values and what they believe is part of their responsibility as parents. Whatever the parents decide, it should be clearly communicated to the teen. For example, if the parents are willing to cover the costs associated with sports but not fund the junk food their kid buys at the games, then they need to be overt about it. This type of discussion evolves over time and requires parents to think about their values as well as set and follow through with financial limits. Anyone who has parented knows that this is sometimes harder than it looks. As their financial advisor, support them in this process and remind them that saying "no" financially is a wonderful gift to give their children, as it teaches them the difference between *wants* and *needs*.

In His Own Words

With teenagers, it can be helpful to sometimes share costs. For instance, if my 13-year-old son needs new basketball sneakers, I may be willing to pay $120 for them. But if he decides he wants the custom Nike ID shoes that cost $175, then he is expected to pay the $55 difference. This is a great way to teach him about wants versus needs. He has to ask himself, "How much do I want the specialized sneakers versus how much do I want $55 in my wallet?" It is a great financial lesson.

—Thomas M. Burke, Jr. vice president, South Shore Bank

During the teen years, encourage your clients to help their children open a personal checking account. This account can be used to deposit any money earned and monetary gifts received. If the child demonstrates good fiscal sense, the parents may even want to consider giving the teen a monthly spending budget for clothes and other expenses that they may previously have covered. This allows the teen to feel a sense of financial independence, to learn to manage income and expenses responsibly, and to master the skill of balancing a checkbook—all important lessons for when they will soon go off to college.

Question: *How do we teach our children not to overextend themselves financially?*

Answer: The best way to teach children not to overextend themselves financially is to have parents who role model healthy financial habits. In addition, encourage your clients to let their older children in on their decision-making process when they are deciding to finance an item. The next time they are trying to decide whether to buy a car using cash or a loan, have the children calculate the interest on the different loans based on the amounts and the term of the loans. Show them with these calculations the cost of credit and how these decisions need to be made carefully. If your clients are in between big purchases, recommend that they sit down with their teens and go over a credit card bill with them. Teach them how to read the bill, calculate the interest due, and see how much money they can save by paying off the balance in full each month.

If your clients have less than stellar credit, they may have a tendency to tell their kids to do one thing, but do another. Gently remind them that actions speak much louder than words. Also encourage them to practice good financial habits alongside their children, as this demonstrates that a person can always decide to be more fiscally responsible.

Question: *How can we educate our children about money and investing?*

Answer: Unfortunately, financial literacy, including lessons on investing money, is not regularly taught in the U.S. school system. Therefore, it is up to the parents to coach their children on the value of investing money to accumulate wealth and how to properly select investments to match one's risk profile and financial objectives. For parents who are financially literate, this is a fairly easy task. However, for many parents who find investing challenging themselves, this is a tall order. This is where you, as their advisor, can provide tremendous value. Host a young adult investing seminar as part of your educational services. Make this event fun by hosting a friendly competition and having each young person pick a stock and follow it over a certain time period. When the time is up, give the teen with the greatest return on investment a prize. If you prefer to do this type of teaching one-on-one, then invite a young person to a meeting with the parents. Teach the same concepts with the entire family in the room. This way, mom and dad get a crash course in investing as well. Finally, if you don't have the time to devote to this type of financial literacy training, find a resource in your area that would be interested in helping out and make a good referral.

Question: *When our children ask the question, "Are we rich?" how do we answer?*

Answer: This question is one that many affluent parents fear. The best advice I can give is to have your clients ask their children what prompted the question and what would it mean to them if the answer was "yes" versus "no." By taking this first step, the parents can gauge what information their child is actually looking for and tailor their response accordingly. It may be that the child is getting teased at school and wants to know what a "rich brat" is. Or it could be that he or she is wondering about different socioeconomic

---

IN HER OWN WORDS

I was giving a workshop on the financially responsible child and one of the women in the audience shared the following: "My son came to me and asked: 'Are we wealthy?' And I answered, "Your father and I are. But you are not." That got a huge laugh and was appreciated by all.

—ELEANOR BLAYNEY, FINANCIAL PLANNER AND FOUNDER
OF DIRECTIONS FOR WOMEN

classes as part of an increased awareness of peers and their wealth. Be honest, give them just enough information to satisfy their curiosity, and, when possible, leave any personal judgments about wealth or poverty out of the discussion. The goal is to make young people feel safe asking questions about money, even if those questions are uncomfortable for the adults.

Question: *How can I start a conversation with my children about an inheritance or upcoming trust distribution?*

Answer: It is important for parents to make sure that the topic of money and wealth is not a taboo one in the household. They can do this by talking with their children about their values and how money is used to express these values from an early age. This way, when a child has a question about the family's wealth, he or she feels no reluctance to bring it up with mom or dad, as money talk is acceptable in the family. When the child does become more curious about his or her inheritance or upcoming trust distribution, encourage your clients to be frank about the family's wealth and the child's inheritance. The concern that many affluent parents have is that the money will act as a demotivator for the child. If the parents actively work at instilling a good work ethic and encourage their children to

---

IN HIS OWN WORDS

My bottom line is, don't shy away from it, but don't make it such a singular experience that it intimidates either parent or child. One good introduction might be to simply ask whether the child is curious about his or her family's [financial] condition. If the answer is "no," let it be for now.

—*TIMOTHY F. LENICHECK, SENIOR VICE PRESIDENT/SENIOR FIDUCIARY OFFICER,*
BOSTON PRIVATE BANK & TRUST COMPANY

pursue their life purpose, this fear is often unfounded. When they are in doubt, encourage them to reach out to you to talk these issues through in more detail based on their specific situation. Let them know that you are only a phone call away.

This list of questions is only the beginning of what couples with children may want your guidance and advice on. Consider creating a handout for your new clients with a list of frequently asked questions on this topic. This lets them know that you are open and willing to help them raise financially thoughtful children. It also can be a tool for opening the door for a discussion on their concerns relative to their family. Together, you can help these couples communicate their values and teach solid financial skills to the next generation.

Summary

Parents want your help when it comes to raising financially savvy children. Offering assistance in this area increases your value to the couple and affords you the opportunity to meet the next generation. You don't have to be an expert on parenting to coach your clients on teaching their children how to manage and talk about money. You just need to tap into your existing knowledge base and figure out how to make these concepts age and developmentally appropriate. Once you master these skills, you will provide great value to your clients as well as to the next generation of wealth holders, who may just decide to hire you when they get old enough to do so.

Your Next Step: Build Your Financial Literacy Library

Helping couples teach their children about money can range from providing them with articles and books on the topic to providing seminars and boot camps for the next generation. To make this part of your practice efficient, take the time to build your financial literacy library now, so that when these requests come in, you are prepared. Here is a list of resources to consider including.

Books

There are a number of good books on this topic for various age groups. For children ages 5 to 18, consider *Raising Financially Fit Children* by Joline Godfrey; for college-aged kids, check out *I Will Teach You to Be Rich* by Ramit Sethi; and for young women, consider *On My Own Two Feet: A Modern Girl's Guide to Personal Finance* by Manisha Thakor and Sharon Kedar.

Websites

Financial literacy training can be an interactive, entertaining experience. Websites such as http://www.SALTmoney.org target young adults ages 18 to 26 and provide customized money management lessons, videos, and fun articles on earning and managing money. Other websites to check out include http://www.feedthepig.org, which focuses on building good saving habits in tweens and teens, and https://www.360financialliteracy.org, which focuses on learners across the life span.

Articles

Write articles on this topic to establish your credibility in this area and provide valuable resources to your clients. You're not a writer? Then ask financial literacy bloggers, educators, and writers for permission to reprint their articles. Make these available in print and also online to meet the different communication needs of different generations.

Tip Sheets

Create single-page tip sheets for parents on this topic. Include your branding and provide this tip sheet in both print and electronic form. Consider addressing topics that speak to your couples. Some ideas include "The Top 10 Money Mistakes Parents Make with Children and How to Avoid Them," "Five Creative Ways to Teach Children About Money," and "How Grandparents Can Teach Their Grandchildren to Save."

Referral Sources

There are boot camps and seminars specifically designed to teach young people about money. Find ones in your area, and then create a list to provide to parents who are interested in giving their children a more in-depth learning experience. Check out the Redwoods Initiative at http://redwoodsinitiative.org if you serve families of substantial wealth, and Independent Means Inc. at http://www .independentmeans.com.

12

Special Issues in Advising Couples

The unexamined life is not worth living.

—Socrates, Greek philosopher

Now that you have learned the essential skills for advising couples, it is time to discuss the potential roadblocks you may face in this work. While there are many factors that can derail the advising process, let's focus on the top three issues that may present in advisory relationships with couples that are longer-term clients. These special issues involve advising couples entrenched in marital discord, couples coping with Alzheimer's disease and dementia, and those suffering from mental health issues and addictions. In each situation, you may be the first professional to recognize a problem or one of many. Either way, knowing the behavioral warning signs, how to use your role as a trusted advisor to help the couples, and how to make a sound referral are paramount. As a caring couple-friendly advisor, you can address these concerns in a manner that fosters trust and shows couples that working in concert with another professional may be the best course of action. Let's take a look at each of these scenarios.

Going Nowhere Fast

Have you ever worked with a couple and thought, "This is going nowhere fast?" If so, it may be that there is more to the couple than meets the eye. Marital problems such as unhealthy communication, lack of trust, infidelity, and abuse may thwart any financial advice and guidance you can provide. As an advisor specializing in working with couples, it is important that you know the signs of marital conflict and how to make a sound referral to a qualified mental health professional when necessary. When asked, many advisors admit that this type of referral is challenging because they fear losing their clients as a result. If you don't notice the proverbial "elephant in the room," however, the chances of this couple moving forward in your financially oriented work in any meaningful way is highly unlikely. Therefore, a well-thought-out referral to a marital counselor will demonstrate that you care about more than the couple's assets and it can help propel the work the couple is doing in your office in the right direction.

> ### In Her Own Words
>
> *The money stuff is not causative of the relationship problems, it's reflective.*
>
> —Shell, 61-year-old money coach "on her last marriage"

How do you know if the couple you are meeting with is just having a bad day or if they are in need of some family and marital counseling? Here are five telltale signs that a couple needs more than a financial advisor.

1. They fight about the same issues each time you meet without any resolution or any movement toward understanding each other's position. For example, the couple rehashes the same fight

about the husband's spending and the wife's frugality at every advisory meeting.

2. One or both partners consistently act in ways that undermine the other partner's involvement in the advising process. For example, a wife calls you after a meeting and asks you to not let her husband know that she called, or a husband purposefully shares important data when his partner is in the bathroom.

3. Despite your efforts to help them resolve their money differences and understand their respective money personalities, the couple stays stuck in struggle and conflict.

4. One or both partners have a mental health issue, such as substance abuse, depression, or gambling, which negatively impacts their financial situation or their ability to follow through with your recommendations.

5. One or both of them disclose that they are contemplating ending the marriage or relationship.

If you notice these signs, it is a good idea to find out if the couple is in therapy already. You would be surprised at how commonplace getting this type of help has become. If they are seeing a therapist, ask permission to talk with this person over the phone. Get this permission in writing, and then ask the marital counselor how you can be most helpful in their healing process. While some therapists are reluctant to collaborate with financial advisors, more professionals are realizing the value of working as a team. If they are not seeing someone, it is time to make a referral to a professional trained in couple and marital counseling.

It is vital that the professional you refer them to is comfortable discussing money issues in relationships and has experience in counseling couples. This is not always easy to find because couples and marital therapy requires a different skill set from individual therapy, and many psychotherapists find talking about money with clients difficult. Just as some financial advisors avoid talking about feelings, many psychotherapists avoid talking about money because of their own ambivalent feelings about wealth. These two professions have a lot to learn from each other.

As a couple-friendly advisor, it is best for you to proactively get to know a few highly qualified marital and family counselors in your area. This not only helps with your marketing efforts, but also facilitates the referral process. If you develop some key relationships with mental health professionals, you don't have to do a lot of extra work when and if you decide to make a referral. If you don't know anyone, I recommend that you network with other financial advisors to find out whom they use. Also visit the Financial Therapy Association website at http://www.financialtherapyassociation.org, visit the American Association for Marriage and Family Therapy website at http://www.aamft.org, or contact a major health insurance plan in your area for names of qualified professionals.

Once you have identified whom you might refer the couple to, approach the conversation with your clients using these five tips:

1. Start by genuinely expressing your concern: "I enjoy working with you two as your financial advisor and want to make sure our time together is beneficial to both of you."

2. Be specific regarding the behaviors that concern you and present this information in a nonjudgmental, empathetic way: "I have noticed in our last few meetings that there was tension between the two of you and you each shared some difficult words. This concerns me, and I am wondering if you need to add another professional to your team to help you communicate more effectively."

3. Normalize their experience: "In my experience, when couples get frustrated, feel stuck in their financial planning meetings, or tensions rise, it is often helpful to refer them to a couples counselor."

4. Don't diagnose: "I believe one or two meetings with a professional who is skilled in helping couples communicate more effectively and resolve differences would benefit you and our work greatly."

5. Stay unattached to the outcome: "What do you think?"

If you are comfortable making a referral of this nature, your clients will be more at ease accepting it. Remember not to diagnose the problem because you are not qualified to do so. Also, the more you can stay unattached to the outcome, the better. Often couples need time and space before they can act on this type of referral. Whether they seek the help you are recommending or not, you have done your duty by expressing your concerns, being clear about what you can and can't help with as their financial advisor, and providing them with a resource to meet their additional needs.

Remember that you can help only couples who are interested in making changes in their financial lives. Some couples will not be able to do this work unless they address the problems in their marriage. Others can move forward without this type of intervention. When you encounter this scenario in your practice, it is best to consult with a trusted colleague, and, if possible, a qualified couples and marital counselor, to decide the best course of action for your clients as well as you.

The Long Goodbye

Conversely to the couples who struggle to stay together, you also find couples who are faced with a long goodbye because one partner is suffering from Alzheimer's disease or dementia. These mental and physical illnesses slowly take away an older client's ability to think clearly, speak articulately, and remember details. Eventually, those afflicted forget their loved ones and become physically incapable of taking care of themselves. Approximately 5.4 million Americans are living with Alzheimer's disease today, with estimates that this number will rise to 16 million by 2050.[1] When you include all forms of dementia,

50 percent of Americans older than age 85 will experience some symptoms, with women twice as likely as men to be stricken.[2] Therefore, the likelihood that you will face this issue in your practice is high.

You can recognize when a client of yours is suffering from Alzheimer's disease or some form of dementia by noting the following indicators.[3]

Intellectual Indicators

◆ Memory loss, known as *amnesia*. This first affects short-term and then long-term memory.
◆ Inability to communicate verbally and in writing, known as *aphasia*. Difficulties in word retrieval and pronunciation often are early warning signs. Some clients completely lose the ability to read and write.
◆ Difficulty performing acts of daily living such as brushing teeth and dressing, known as *apraxia*.
◆ Inability to correctly interpret signals from the five senses, known as *agnosia*. Afflicted person may not recognize familiar people or correctly read their own bodily cues such as fullness in the stomach or bladder.

Emotional Indicators

◆ Personality changes
◆ Depression, agitation, and irritability
◆ Hallucinations, paranoia, and delusions with disease progression

Many elderly people impacted by these intellectual and emotional indicators go to great lengths to hide these deficits from professionals and family members alike. This relates to the shame many clients feel about being sick, even though dementia is not within a person's control. Furthermore, denial runs high for the spouses, life partners, and children of these clients. Part of the reason is that a change in behavior can be fairly apparent to someone like you who interacts with the client on an annual or biannual basis, but can be almost unnoticeable on a day-to-day basis. Also, many partners are unconsciously protecting themselves from coming to terms with their partner's illness and what it means for their lives.

IN HIS OWN WORDS

In retrospect, I would have been more proactive in getting resources to help care for my elderly parents. For too long I was trying to be Superman in dealing with many varied issues (including dementia) related to my parents' care.... Don't fool yourself into thinking the needs of your elderly parents are temporary or will decrease in the future. That has not been my experience.

—SCOTT, 48-YEAR-OLD MARRIED FATHER OF TWO AND CAREGIVER

The best course of action for you, as the couple's financial advisor, is to be proactive. However, this is not always possible. Therefore, keep the following steps in mind when this couple client issue comes to your attention.

Step 1: Documentation

Make sure all your clients, regardless of age, have up-to-date living wills, healthcare proxies, powers of attorney, and related estate-planning documents, with accurate beneficiaries listed in all their insurance and related policies. This ensures that your couple clients are prepared from a legal standpoint should they unfortunately have to face this illness.

Step 2: Meetings

As your clients age, consider meeting them on a more regular basis and conducting at least one meeting a year at their home. This allows you to notice any changes in their cognitive or emotional health and also gives you a window into their daily world. Often clients with dementia will live in disarray as they lose the ability to organize their daily lives, which is evident when they let you into their homes.

Step 3: Notice

Keep an eye out for the symptoms of dementia in your clients and follow up on any concerns you may have with your clients' partners. Even if they don't confirm your suspicion, you can document in your notes that you discussed it and have also planted a seed in the partner's mind that may help with denial if indeed there is a problem.

Step 4: Refer

If your suspicions are confirmed or if you are fairly certain that there has been a change in the cognitive ability of one or both partners to manage their financial life, make a referral to a specialist in the area of Alzheimer's disease or dementia. This communicates to your clients that you care enough to encourage them to be evaluated. Given your role as a financial advisor, you can't diagnose your clients, but you can strongly recommend that they seek the help of a trained medical professional to determine the cause of these behavioral changes. Reassure your clients that you may be wrong, but you would like to err on the side of safety. (See the resource guide in the back of this book for organizations that can provide you with or refer you to professionals who offer this type of specialized assessment.)

Step 5: Support

If a diagnosis is made, support your clients in mitigating the financial consequences of the illness. According to the Alzheimer's Disease Education and Referral Center, you should recommend that clients execute these documents prior to mental decline:[4]

- A living will to communicate the person's wishes for how medical treatment should be handled
- A durable power of attorney to designate who will make healthcare decisions when the client is no longer able to

do so and so that a designated person can easily handle the sufferer's financial affairs

◆ A will to address asset distribution

If you have already completed Step 1, this task will be fairly straightforward and familiar to your clients. In many instances, you will work with their legal counsel to make sure that these documents are drawn up correctly and kept current.

When working with clients who are still mentally capable of making financial decisions, but are slowing down cognitively, it is important to treat them with respect. You need to speak slowly, be patient if it takes them some time to find the right words to answer your questions, and communicate any information in small, bite-size pieces. Write any recommendations or action steps down on a piece of paper, and give a copy to the client and the partner. Whenever possible, have the client's partner or adult children in the room. This allows the client to still be actively involved in the meetings and ensures that the information communicated will be retained. Finally, recognize that a time will eventually come when it is no longer prudent for the client to meet with you. Make this determination along with the partner and caregivers, and know in your heart that you have done some good work to help this couple in a time of need.

IN HER OWN WORDS

As someone who recently lost her mother after a 10-year battle with Alzheimer's disease, I can assure you that the goodbye process is long, and at times painful. Ironically, it can also be filled with joy, laughter, and warmth as you learn to connect with the person in new ways.

—KATRINA, 54-YEAR-OLD MARRIED PROFESSIONAL

In addition to the financial advice and guidance you can provide at this time, it is also helpful to support the client's partner and children during this difficult transition. If you have already met the next generation, it can facilitate the process of supporting the client because all the players are familiar. If not, this is often a good time to reach out, if they have not done so already.

In the end, coping with this illness requires a team approach that includes doctors, nurses, and home healthcare workers, as well as estate attorneys and financial advisors. You play an important role in supporting the couple in planning for and eventually saying their long goodbye.

Too Much of a Good Thing: Gambling, Spending, and Addiction

Sometimes clients can't get enough of a good thing. They may over-shop, gamble, or blow their hard-earned cash on drugs and alcohol. In fact, mental illness affects approximately 26.2 percent of Americans ages 18 and older, or 57.7 million people.[5] Therefore, if you have a successful advising practice, you are statistically likely to have someone on your book of business with one of these problems.

What do you do if you notice that a client is coming to meetings drunk or high? Or if you sense that the client's wife is trying to curtail her spending, but just can't get it under control? Or if you know that the husband is blowing his retirement savings at the casino downtown? The couple-friendly thing to do is to gently address your concerns and help the client in need get help for his or her mental health issue.

Making this type of referral can be emotionally difficult for you as the advisor, but you don't have to act alone. In fact, if you suspect a client is faced with one of these problems, I recommend that you contact a mental health professional with this specialty. Discuss the behaviors that concern you and get some recommendations on how to best approach the situation. In addition, learn more about the illness. For gambling addictions, visit the Gamblers Anonymous website at http://www.gamblersanonymous.org; for substance abuse and drug addictions, visit the Alcoholics Anonymous website at http://www.aa.org or the Narcotics Anonymous website at http://www.na.org/; and for spending problems, visit the Shopaholic No More website at http://www.shopaholicnomore.com/. All of these resources have lists of signs and symptoms, information for the partners of those who are suffering, and referrals to qualified mental health professional or treatment centers.

Armed with this information, use the five tips described in the "Going Nowhere Fast" section of this chapter. Again avoid diagnosing the problem and just stick to the behaviors you notice that are worrisome. For example, if you suspect the wife has a drinking problem, you may say something like, "I notice that you are spending a lot on wine, and as a result you are not keeping to the spending plan we discussed at your last visit. I wonder if it might make sense to add a member to your financial planning team who is skilled in looking at spending behaviors and works with clients to help them change unwanted habits." Notice that you are not pointing a finger or calling the client an alcoholic. You are simply expressing concern about her behaviors and how they impact her financial life. Offering a referral is in the client's best interest, but it also is in yours because you are clearly communicating the limits to your expertise.

Summary

Working as a couple-friendly advisor requires you to have financial knowledge and expertise plus a desire to help your clients address all aspects of their lives. Sometimes this results in your initiating an uncomfortable but necessary conversation about what you have noticed in your clients' behaviors and how a referral to a medical or mental health professional is warranted. With time and practice, these conversations become easier to engage in. Often what you fear—alienating a client—is unfounded. In the end clients who know that you care about more than just their assets remain loyal to the professionals who helped them out at a time of need.

Your Next Step: Take One Step Out of Your Comfort Zone

All of us have a place where we are most comfortable professionally. For you, as an advisor, it may be meeting with clients, discussing risk tolerance, or crunching numbers. From time to time, however, you will be asked to step outside this comfort zone to meet the needs of your clients. To do this effectively, you should determine what is in your comfort zone and how you can take one step outside of it to help your couple clients who are in need.

On a piece of paper, draw a large circle. Then draw four circles inside this original one, each slightly smaller in size. In the end you will have five concentric circles that resemble the ripples in a pond that are created when you toss a stone into it. Now label the smallest circle "my comfort zone," the next one, "one step outside," then "two steps outside," and so on, until you label the largest circle, "way outside my comfort zone." Next, list all the activities you professionally engage in where you feel confident and at ease in the circle marked "my comfort zone." Then list all the activities you find overwhelming, scary, and outside of your area of expertise in the circle marked "way outside my comfort zone." Now that you have both extremes identified, write down where each of the following activities would go on your comfort zone map.

___ Making a mental health referral
___ Making a drug and alcohol referral
___ Making a marriage counseling referral
___ Talking to a client about my concerns regarding possible dementia
___ Meeting with a caregiver of a client with Alzheimer's disease
___ Helping a client who gambles find treatment

___ Talking to a couple who has a special needs child

___ Referring a client with early stages of dementia to an estate attorney

Feel free to add other activities to your map that you feel are applicable.

Once your comfort zone chart is completed, review it. Consider the activities that are one step outside your comfort zone. Could you dip your toe into the water and give them a try next quarter? For example, if you find networking with a marriage and family therapist to be one step outside your comfort zone, why not arrange a meeting in the next month to do so? This is a nice way to gently push yourself to take an extra step on behalf of your clients, while respecting your limits. The goal is to try the activities that are slightly anxiety provoking as a way of growing professionally and leaving the ones that cause a complete panic attack to other professionals.

Now create a list of the three steps you will take in the next quarter to step out of your comfort zone. Share this list with a trusted colleague or coach. Having someone to be accountable to will help you take these small, calculated risks.

	Action Step	Target Completion Date	Completion Date
Example	*Visit gamblers anonymous website*	*One month from today*	
1.			
2.			
3.			

Conclusion

As an industry, we need to do a much better job serving couples. This entails being open-minded and curious about how the modern couple makes, manages, and invests their money. It also requires a commitment to provide more training and mentoring relative to the many skills required to advise partners effectively. Currently, this type of education is left up to the individual advisor's initiative. The unspoken (and sometimes spoken) message is that clients' assets matter more than their attitudes and emotions about money. The way I see it, you can't have one without the other. Thought leaders in the field of behavioral economics are providing the research to support the importance of assessing investors' behaviors for outcomes. And it is time that the financial services industry follows suit and provides you, the advisor, with practical skills and tactics too.

For there to be true change in the financial services industry, the emotional side of finance needs to be seen as a necessary and vital part of the equation. The label of *soft* allows too many professionals to ignore the invaluable data that emotions and relationship dynamics provide to the planning process. Instead of treating clients as if they were void of feelings, let's embrace their humanness and make it okay to discuss the underlying thoughts and beliefs that influence their financial habits. Some in the industry have already done so with great success. Others are still fighting the tide. But clients want and value advisors who are curious about their unique life experiences, money personalities, family histories, and values. So let's give our clients what they want.

My passion for better serving women led me to write this book on advising couples. Through this process, I am reminded of how powerful women are economically and how far they have come. It is an exciting time to be a woman business owner and to be working in an industry that is finally giving female clients the attention they deserve. It is also important to note that, similarly to the way many women feel neglected by advisors, many men are being overlooked too. These men are not the stereotypical money-motivated types. Instead, they are husbands or partners who relish their mates' success and allow them to take the financial reins for the family. In the same way that, women were not invited to the advising table in the past, these modern men are being left out as well. No matter what the gender of the client, it is important for the financial health of the couple and in the best interest of your business to make sure both partners are actively involved. This takes more time and effort on your part, but it is the only way you can operate as a truly couple-friendly advisor.

Since you are reading this book, I realize that you are the exception to the rule. You know that the investment in better serving couples comes with a high return. By paying attention to the nuances and psychology of couplehood, you are more prepared to offer financial solutions that work. As a result, many of your couple clients will amass more wealth, raise more financially intelligent children, and see you as their trusted advisor for life. This type of advising requires you to be proficient in the essential skills for advising couples outlined in this book. You need to master the art of building a solid foundation of trust, uncovering money mindsets, balancing gender differences, managing conflict, and facilitating lasting change. And for those couples who are parents, you have a unique opportunity to empower them to raise a financially savvy next generation.

Writing a book is a big project, full of ups and downs and life lessons. *How to Give Financial Advice to Couples* was no exception. Professionally, I was reminded of how diverse the definition of couplehood is, how clients' sexual orientation can influence their view of the world in subtle ways, and how men talk in headlines and women talk in stories. Personally, I discovered how to be a better financial partner in my marriage, and how sometimes this means not doing it *my way*. However, the biggest lesson I learned is that I am just as passionate about empowering couples financially as I am about empowering women financially.

As an advisor, you play a vital role in helping couples talk more openly and honestly about money. Your work to improve their financial communication, insight, and health is admirable. In the end, what a wonderful world it would be if all advisors were as couple-friendly as you!

Notes

Introduction

1. K. Wojnar and C. Meek, "Women's Views of Wealth and the Planning Process: It's Their Values That Matter, Not Just Their Value," *Advisor Perspectives*, 5, no. 9 (March 2011): 2, http://www.advisorperspectives .com/newsletters11/pdfs/Womens_Views_of_Wealth_and_the_Planning_ Process.pdf.

Chapter 1

1. Hanna Rosin, *The End of Men: And the Rise of Women* (New York: Penguin Group, 2012), 48.
2. Liza Mundy, *The Richer Sex: How the New Majority of Female Breadwinners Is Transforming Sex, Love and Family* (New York: Simon & Schuster, 2012), 6.
3. Bridget Brennan, *Why She Buys: The New Strategy for Reaching the World's Most Powerful Consumers* (New York: Crown Business, 2009), 4.
4. K. Wojnar and C. Meek, "Women's Views of Wealth and the Planning Process: It's Their Values That Matter, Not Just Their Value," *Advisor Perspectives* 5, no. 9 (March 2011): 2, http://www.advisorperspectives .com/newsletters11/pdfs/Womens_Views_of_Wealth_and_the_Planning_ Process.pdf.
5. Mark Solheim, "What You Need to Know About Couples & Money," *Kiplinger's Personal Finance* 62, no. 6 (June 2008): 95.
6. The State of Our Unions, "Social Indicators of Marital Health & Well-Being: Trends of the Past Five Decades," http://www.stateofourunions .org/2011/social_indicators.php.
7. Jim McConville, "Fidelity Guide Helps Advisors Talk with Couples Approaching Retirement," *Financial Advisor*, http://www.fa-mag.com/ news/fidelity-guide-helps-advisors-talk-with-couples-approaching -retirement-9191.html.

Chapter 2

1. CESI Debt Solutions, "National Survey Reveals Truth About Marriage and Credit Cards," CESI Debt Solutions, http://www.cesidebtsolutions. org/downloads/marriageanddebt.pdf.
2. Jessica Dickler, "Lying to Your Spouse About Money? Join the Club," CNNMoney, http://money.cnn.com/2012/05/04/pf/spouse-money/ index.htm.
3. Liza Mundy, *The Richer Sex: How the New Majority of Female Breadwinners Is Transforming Sex, Love and Family* (New York: Simon & Schuster, 2012), 53.

4. Ibid., 52.

5. Ibid, 39.

6. Ramit Sethi, "13 Stunning Differences in How Men and Women Think About Money," I Will Teach You to Be Rich, http://www .iwillteachyoutoberich.com/blog/13-stunning-differences-in-how-men -and-women-think-about-money/.

Chapter 3

1. Margaret Shapiro, "Money: A Therapeutic Tool for Couples Therapy," *Family Process* 46, no. 3 (September 2007): 279–291.

Chapter 4

1. New York Life, "New Solutions for Non-Traditional Families Facing Traditional Financial Concerns," New York Life, http://www.newyorklife .com/nyl/v/index.jsp?vgnextoid=875bce42249d2210a2b3019d221024301 cacRCRD.

2. W. Bradford Wilcox, ed., "The State of Our Unions: Marriage in America 2011," The National Marriage Project (2011): 75, http:// nationalmarriageproject.org/wp-content/uploads/2012/05/Union_2011.pdf.

3. Scott M. Stanley and Lindsey A. Einhorn, "Hitting Pay Dirt: Comment on 'Money as a Therapeutic Tool for Couples Therapy,'" *Family Process* 46, no. 3 (September 2007): 295.

4. Casey E. Copen, Kimberly Daniels, Jonathan Vespa, and William D. Mosher, "National Health Statistics Report: First Marriages in the United States: Data From the 2006–2010 National Survey of Family Growth," Centers for Disease Control and Prevention, http://www.cdc.gov/nchs/ data/nhsr/nhsr049.pdf.

5. David Popenoe and Barbara D. Whitehead, "The State of Our Unions: The Social Health of Marriage in America 1999," The National Marriage Project (1999): 10, http://www.stateofourunions.org/pdfs/SOOU1999.pdf.

6. Ibid., 14.

7. Wilcox, "The State of Our Unions," 69, 73.

8. State Street Global Advisors, "Capitalizing on the HNW Women Opportunity: How to Connect with Your Clients," SPDR University, http://www.spdru.com/category/communicating-with-clients/#/content/ capitalizing-on-the-hnw-women-opportunity-how-to-connect-with -your-clients.

9. Ibid.

10. K. Wojnar and C. Meek, "Women's Views of Wealth and the Planning Process: It's Their Values That Matter, Not Just Their Value," *Advisor Perspectives* 5, no. 9 (March 2011): 2, http://www.advisorperspectives .com/newsletters11/pdfs/Womens_Views_of_Wealth_and_the_Planning_ Process.pdf.

11. H. Pordeli and P. Wynkoop, "The Economic Impact of Women-Owned Businesses in the United States" (research report, Center for Women's Business Research, McLean, VA, October 2009), http://www.nwbc.gov/sites/default/files/economicimpactstu.pdf.

12. Center for Women's Business Research, "Key Facts About Women-Owned Businesses" (Women Entrepreneurs Institute, January 2009), http://www.women-entrepreneurs.org/PDF/2009_Key_Facts.pdf.

13. Pordeli and Wynkoop, "The Economic Impact of Women-Owned Businesses."

14. Hanna Rosin, *The End of Men: And the Rise of Women* (New York: Penguin Group, 2012).

15. TD Ameritrade, "Life Stage and Money Management Survey," May 2010, http://files.shareholder.com/downloads/AMTD/2310847314x0x370840/ca349d0c-efa3-4287-a746-44e5a0026a84/LifestagefindingsFINAL_042710.pdf.

16. Christine Moriarty and Kathleen Burns Kingsbury, "Couples and Money: Facts, Fiction and Feelings" (lecture, FPA of Massachusetts Symposium, Boston, MA, May 23, 2012).

17. Gregory M. Herek, "Facts About Homosexuality and Mental Health," UC Davis Psychology Department, http://psychology.ucdavis.edu/rainbow/html/facts_mental_health.html. Accessed February 1, 2013.

18. Richard F. Stolz, "Estate Planning for Unmarried Couples: What Financial Planners Need to Know," *Journal of Financial Planning* 25, no. 2 (February 2012): 20–24.

19. Suzanne Slater, interview by author, January 3, 2013.

20. Freedom to Marry, "States," November 2012, http://www.freedomtomarry.org/states/.

21. Huffpost Politics, "Supreme Court on Gay Marriage: Prop 8, DOMA to Receive Hearings," *HuffPolitics Blog*, December 7, 2012, http://www.huffingtonpost.com/2012/12/07/supreme-court-gay-marriage_n_2218441.html.

22. Caren Chesler, "With Gay Marriage Comes Gay Divorce," IBLN Designs, http://www.iblndesigns.com/caren/article33.htm.

23. Suzanne Slater, interview by author, January 3, 2013.

24. Savita Iyer-Ahrestani, "The Challenges of Advising Same Sex Couples," *Bank Investment Consultant* 19, no. 11 (November 2011): 28–32.

25. Suzanne Slater, interview by author, January 3, 2013.

26. Ibid.

27. Pew Research Center, "A Portrait of Stepfamilies," Pew Research Social & Demographic Trends, January 2011, http://www.pewsocialtrends.org/2011/01/13/a-portrait-of-stepfamilies/.

28. Ibid.

29. Emily Bouchard, interview by author, January 3, 2013.

30. Stephanie Sharp, interview by author, February 12, 2013.

Chapter 5

1. Margaret Shapiro, LCSW, "Money: A Therapeutic Tool for Couples," *Family Process* 46, no. 3 (September 2007): 279–291.

2. Danny Deza, "How Love Changes Your Body Chemistry," *Health Magazine*, http://www.health.com/health/gallery/0,20568672_2,00.html.

3. Faith Fuller, cofounder of CRR Global, e-mail message to author, January 28, 2013.

4. Shell Tain, interview by author, November 16, 2012.

5. The State of Our Unions 2012, "Social Indicators of Marital Health & Well-Being: Trends of the Past Five Decades," http://www.stateofourunions .org/2011/social_indicators.php.

6. Linda Skogrand, Alena C. Johnson, Amanda M. Horrocks, and John DeFrain, "Financial Management Practices of Couples with Great Marriages," *Journal of Family and Economic Issues* 32, no. 1 (March 2011): 27–35.

7. John Gottman and Robert Levenson, "The Timing of Divorce: Predicting When a Couple Will Divorce over a 14-Year Period," *Journal of Marriage and Family*, 62 (August 2000): 737.

8. Diana Mansfield, interview by author, November 24, 2012.

9. Joan D. Atwood, "Couples and Money: The Last Taboo," *American Journal of Family Therapy* 40, no. 1 (January 2012): 1–19.

10. Ibid.

11. Wendy Wang and Rich Morin, "Home for the Holidays . . . and Every Other Day," Pew Research Social & Demographic Trends, November 24, 2009, www.pewsocialtrends.org/2009/11/24/ home-for-the-holidays-and-every-other-day/.

12. Kim Parker, "The Boomerang Generation," Pew Research Social & Demographic Trends, March 15, 2012, http://www.pewsocialtrends .org/2012/03/15/the-boomerang-generation/.

13. Joline Godfrey and David Wegbreit,"The Launch: How Great Families Develop the Next Generation," Summatis, November 2010, https://www .summitas.com/system/files/secure/Independent%20Means%20-%20 The%20Launch.pdf.

14. Ibid.

15. Kim Parker and Eileen Patten, "The Sandwich Generation: Rising Financial Burdens for Middle-Aged Americans," Pew Research Social & Demographic Trends, January 30, 2013, http://www.pewsocialtrends .org/2013/01/30/the-sandwich-generation.

16. Ibid.

17. Sally Abrahms, "Life After Divorce," AARP, June 6, 2012, http://www .aarp.org/home-family/friends-family/info-05-2012/life-after-divorce.html.

18. Mitch Anthony, "Practice Retirement®: A New Way to Talk to Your Clients About the Retirement Transition" (lecture, TD Ameritrade Institutional Conference, San Diego, CA, January 31, 2013).

19. Ibid.

20. Abrahms, "Life After Divorce."
21. Dorian Mintzer, interview by author, November 25, 2012.
22. "Financial Responsibilities in Marriage: Financial Infidelity: Love Honor and Disclose: Tips to Run Marriage Like a Company," Divorce360, www .divorce360.com/articles/print_view.aspx?artid=1459.
23. Gail Liberman, "The Changing World of Marital Law," *Financial Advisor*, July 1, 2003, http://www.fa-mag.com/news/article-728.html.
24. Tim Maurer, interview by author, January 22, 2013.

Chapter 6

1. Carol Kinsey Goman, PhD, "Seven Seconds to Make a First Impression," *Forbes*, February 13, 2011, http://www.forbes.com/sites/ carolkinseygoman/2011/02/13/seven-seconds-to-make-a-first-impression.
2. Denise Federer, PhD, interview by author, November 10, 2012.
3. TD Ameritrade Institutional, "Establishing Trust in the Advisor-Client Relationship," March 2011, *InvestmentNews*, http://www.investmentnews .com/assets/docs/CI7746021.PDF.
4. Ibid.
5. Laura Varas, interview by author, January 11, 2013.
6. Kathleen Burns Kingsbury, *How to Give Financial Advice to Women: Attracting and Retaining High-Net-Worth Female Clients* (New York: McGraw-Hill, 2013).
7. Carol Kinsey Goman, PhD, "Ten Body Language Mistakes Women Leaders Make," *Forbes*, July 12, 2010, http://www.forbes. com/2010/07/12/body-language-mistakes-women-forbes-woman -leadership-authority.html.
8. Kol Birke, interview by author, December 20, 2011.

Chapter 7

1. K. Wojnar and C. Meek, "Women's Views of Wealth and the Planning Process: It's Their Values That Matter, Not Just Their Value," *Advisor Perspectives*, 5, no. 9 (March, 2011): 2, http://www.advisorperspectives .com/newsletters11/pdfs/Womens_Views_of_Wealth_and_the_Planning_ Process.pdf.
2. Michael Silverstein, Kosuke Kato, and Pia Tischhauser, "Women Want More (in Financial Services)," Boston Consulting Group, 2009, https://www.bcgperspectives.com/content/articles/ women_want_more_in_financial_services/.
3. State Street Global Advisors, "Capitalizing on the HNW Women Opportunity: How to Connect with Your Clients," SPDR University, http://www.spdru.com/category/communicating-with-clients/#/content/ capitalizing-on-the-hnw-women-opportunity-how-to-connect-with-your -clients.

4. H. Pordeli and P. Wynkoop, "The Economic Impact of Women-Owned Businesses in the United States" (research report, Center for Women's Business Research, McLean, VA, October 2009), http://www.nwbc.gov/sites/default/files/economicimpactstu.pdf.

5. Bridget Brennan, *Why She Buys: The New Strategy for Reaching the World's Most Powerful Consumers* (New York: Crown Business, 2009), 4.

6. Louann Brizendine, *The Female Brain* (New York: Broadway Books, 2006).

7. "Perspectives on Gender & Personality," *On Wall Street,* no. 9 (September 2012): A12.

8. Michael Fischer, "Gender Gap Exposed in Millionaires' Financial Decision Making," AdvisorOne, November 30, 2012, http://www.advisorone.com/2012/11/30/gender-gap-exposed-in-millionaires-financial-decis.

9. Heather Ettinger and Eileen O'Connor, *Women of Wealth: Why Does the Financial Services Industry Still Not Hear Them?* (Cleveland: Family Wealth Advisory Council, 2011): 24.

10. Prudential Research Group, "Financial Experience and Behaviors Among Women: 2012–2013 Prudential Research Study" (Newark: Prudential Financial, 2012).

11. E. Blayney, "Empowering, Educating, and Engaging Women Clients," *Journal of Financial Planning* 23, no. 10 (October 2010): 48–50, 52–55.

12. Allianz Life Insurance, "Report on Women, Money and Power" (Minneapolis: Allianz, 2006).

13. Ann Woodyard and Cliff Robb, "Financial Knowledge and the Gender Gap," *Journal of Financial Therapy* 3, no. 1 (2012): 1.

14. Brad M. Barbar and Terrance Odean, "Boys Will Be Boys: Gender, Overconfidence and Common Stock Investment," *Quarterly Journal of Economics* 116, no. 1 (February 2001): 289.

15. Barclays Wealth and Ledbury Research, "Understanding the Female Economy: The Role of Gender in Financial Decision Making and Succession Planning for the Next Generation," Barclays Wealth, 2011, http://www.barclayswealth.com/Images/BW_Female_Client_Group_report.PDF.

16. Ibid., 3.

17. Ettinger and O'Connor, *Women of Wealth.*

18. Barclays Wealth and Ledbury Research, "Understanding the Female Economy," 12.

19. University Communications, "Which Is the Chattier Gender," *UANews,* July 2, 2007, http://uanews.org/story/which-chattier-gender.

20. Brizendine, *The Female Brain.*

21. Carol Kinsey Goman, PhD, "Ten Body Language Mistakes Women Leaders Make," *Forbes,* July 12, 2010, http://www.forbes.com/2010/07/12/body-language-mistakes-women-forbes-woman-leadership-authority.html.

22. Ettinger and O'Connor, *Women of Wealth.*

Chapter 8

1. Carol Anderson and Deanna L. Sharpe, "The Efficacy of Life Planning Communication Tasks in Developing Successful Planner-Client Relationships," *Journal of Financial Planning* 21, no. 6 (June 2008): 67.
2. Brad Klontz, PsyD, and Ted Klontz, PhD, *Mind over Money: overcoming the Money Disorders That Threaten Our Financial Health* (New York: Broadway Books, 2009), 109.
3. Ibid., 110–111.
4. Financial DNA, "Financial Personality Discovery: DNA Financial Performance Report for Chris Coddington," http://www.dnabehavior.com/Financial%20Performance%20Report_v1.9.pdf.
5. Center for Applications of Psychological Type, "Jung's Theory of Psychological Types and the MBTI® Instrument," http://www.capt.org/take-mbti-assessment/mbti-overview.htm. Accessed January 31, 2013.
6. Robert P. Hanlon, Jr., "The Use of Typology in Financial Planning," *Journal of Financial Planning* 13, no. 7 (July 2000): 96–112.
7. Jennifer Selby Long, "Are You the Wealthy Type?," The Selby Group, 2007, http://www.selbygroup.com/docs/Wealthy_Types_0107.pdf.
8. Kathy Kolbe, "Kolbe A Index™: Actions Based on Instincts," Kolbe Corp., https://www.kolbe.com/pdfassets/Kolbe_A_Index.pdf.
9. Bill Harris and Paula Harris, interview by author, November 23, 2012.
10. Joline Godfrey, *Raising Financially Fit Kids* (Berkeley: Ten Speed Press, 2003), 15–19.
11. Olivia Mellan, *Money Harmony: Resolving Money Conflicts in Your Life and Relationships* (New York: Walker & Company, 1995), 71–96.
12. Deborah L. Price, *Money Magic: Unleashing Your True Potential for Prosperity and Fulfillment* (Novato, CA: New World Library, 2003), 33–56.

Chapter 9

1. Wisdom Quotes, "Mary Parker Follett Quotes," http://www.wisdomquotes.com/authors/mary-parker-follett. Accessed February 15, 2013.
2. John Guttmann, PhD, Julia Schwartz Gotman, PhD, and Joan Declaire, *10 Lessons to Transform Your Marriage* (New York: Crown Publishing, 2006).
3. Ibid.
4. Shell Tain, interview by author, November 17, 2012.

Chapter 10

1. James O. Prochaska and Carlo C. DiClemente, "Stages and Processes of Self-Change of Smoking Toward an Integrative Model of Change," *Journal of Consulting and Clinical Psychology* 51, no. 3 (June 1983): 390–395.

2. Harriet Lerner, *The Dance of Anger: The Woman's Guide to Changing the Patterns of Intimate Relationships* (New York: Perennial Currents, 2005), 15.

Chapter 11

1. Capgemini and Merrill Lynch Global Wealth Management, "World Wealth Report: 2011," Merrill Lynch, http://www.ml.com/media/114235 .pdf.
2. Kathleen Burns Kingsbury and James Grubman, PhD, "Ensuring Success in Wealth Transfers: Involving and Preparing the Beneficiary," *Investments & Wealth Monitor* (September/October 2010): 14–17.
3. Joline Godfrey, *Raising Financially Fit Kids* (Berkeley: Ten Speed Press, 2003).

Chapter 12

1. Alzheimer's Association, "2012 Alzheimer's Disease Facts and Figures," Factsheet, March 2012, http://www.alz.org/documents_custom/2012_ facts_figures_fact_sheet.pdf.
2. Steve Starns, "Is Your Firm Prepared for Alzheimer's? How to Communicate with Clients with Dementia," *Journal of Financial Planning* 23, no. 12 (December 2010): 62.
3. Alzheimer's Foundation of America, "About Alzheimer's: Symptoms," http://www.alzfdn.org/AboutAlzheimers/symptoms.html. Accessed February 27, 2013.
4. Alzheimer's Disease Education and Referral (ADEAR) Center, "Legal and Financial Planning for People with Alzheimer's Disease," Home Care Network, Inc., http://www.sjrrn.com/hcn-pdfs/Legal%20and%20 Financial%20Planning%20Alzheimers.pdf. Accessed February 27, 2013.
5. National Institute of Mental Health, "The Numbers Count: Mental Disorders in America," http://www.nimh.nih.gov/health/publications/ the-numbers-count-mental-disorders-in-america/index.shtml. Accessed February 27, 2013.

Couple-Friendly Resource Guide

What follows are couple-friendly resources categorized by topic. These books, online resources, and organizations provide valuable information for you and the couples you advise.

Aging
Books

Learning to Speak Alzheimer's: A Groundbreaking Approach for Everyone Dealing with the Disease
By Joanne Koenig Coste
The author offers a practical approach to the emotional well-being of both patients and caregivers that emphasizes relating to patients in their own reality. This book offers hundreds of practical tips including how to cope with the diagnosis and adjust to the disease's progression, and how to help the patient talk about the illness.

The 36-Hour Day: A Family Guide to Caring for People Who Have Alzheimer Disease, Related Dementias, and Memory Loss
By Nancy L. Mace and Peter V. Rabins
For more than 30 years, this book has been the trusted bible for families affected by dementia disorders. Now completely revised and updated, this guide features the latest information on the causes of dementia, managing the early stages of dementia, the prevention of dementia, and finding appropriate living arrangements for the person who has dementia when home care is no longer an option. A section on financial issues is included.

Organizations

Alzheimer's Association
http://www.alz.org
Founded in 1980, the Alzheimer's Association advances research to end Alzheimer's disease and dementia while enhancing care for those

living with the disease. The website offers educational resources, financial and legal information, support group listings, and referrals to treatment facilities across the country.

Boomers and Beyond Special Interest Group

http://www.revolutionizeretirement.com

Revolutionize Retirement, founded by Dorian Mintzer, PhD, coauthor of *The Couple's Retirement Puzzle*. It is a forum for interdisciplinary professionals to explore positive, creative, and successful aging. Meetings occur via teleconference the first and third Tuesday of each month at noon EST. For more information, go to the website and sign up in the "Boomers and Beyond" section.

Boston University Alzheimer's Disease Center

http://www.bu.edu/alzresearch/

The Boston University Alzheimer's Disease Center aims to reduce the human and economic costs of Alzheimer's disease through the advancement of knowledge. They are associated with Boston University Neurology Associates, which offers a full spectrum of neurological care with a specialty in dementia.

Couples and Family Dynamics

Books

The Couple's Retirement Puzzle: 10 Must-Have Conversations for Transition to the Second Half of Life

By Roberta Taylor and Dorian Mintzer

Written as a self-help book, this can also be used by financial advisors to facilitate conversations between partners as they approach this stage of life. Filled with exercises and information, this is a great resource for you and your clients alike.

Men Are from Mars, Women Are from Venus: The Classic Guide to Understanding the Opposite Sex

By John Gray

A classic book on couples and communication originally published more than a decade ago, it was last updated in 2004. It contains tips, tools, and proven strategies based on the author's experience as a well-respected marriage counselor.

Money Harmony: A Road Map for Individuals and Couples
By Oliva Mellan and Sherry Christie
With an innovative program developed by Mellan to help individuals and couples resolve their money conflicts, this book teaches you how to gain insight into your own money style by evaluating the impact of childhood experiences on your current money attitudes and behaviors.

The Heart of Money
By Deborah Price
This book educates readers on how money issues have long been the number one cause of relationship disharmony and divorce and offers couples tips and tools for resolving these differences. She is also the author of *Money Magic*, mentioned in the following "Financial Psychology" section.

Organizations

Bowen Center for the Study of the Family
http://www.thebowencenter.org
The mission of the Bowen Center is to lead the development of Bowen family systems theory into a science of human behavior and to assist individuals, families, communities, and organizations in solving major life problems through understanding and improving human relationships. They offer training for financial advisors as well as therapists, coaches, and consultants.

CRR Global
http://www.crrglobal.com/
CRR Global offers an advanced coach training program specifically designed to assist coaches in working with couples, families, and organizational systems.

Family Firm Institute, Inc.

http://www.ffi.org

The Family Firm Institute is the leading membership association worldwide for professionals who service the family enterprise field. The website has a list of local chapters, online resources, and articles, and a listing of professionals specializing in working with affluent families.

Financial Literacy

Books

I Will Teach You to Be Rich

By Ramit Sethi

This book contains a six-week personal finance course for 20- to 35-year-olds. The author provides a practical approach and delivers information in a non-judgmental style.

On My Own Two Feet: A Modern Girl's Guide to Personal Finance

By Manisha Thakor and Sharon Kedar

Through the use of their financial planning experience, Thakor and Kedar teach young women what they need to know about saving and investing in language that is user-friendly.

Raising Financially Fit Kids

By Joline Godfrey

Providing a developmental map that covers 10 specific money skills, this book teaches children to master these skills by the time they reach age 18 and to become financially secure adults. The map gives parents a step-by-step approach to helping their kids become habitual savers, smart money managers, and responsible decision makers.

Websites

SALT Money

http://www.saltmoney.org

SALT Money offers young adults savvy tips on everything from getting a student loan, to making a big purchase, to talking to their parents about money. Learning tools include games, quizzes, videos, articles, and lots of cool stuff to make learning about finance fun.

Feed the Pig
http://www.feedthepig.com
A fun financial literacy website focused on helping people save more responsibly. Sign up for weekly reminders and tips on how to save more and spend less.

360 Degrees of Financial Literacy
http://www.360financialliteracy.org
This website is broken down into financial lessons according to where the user is in his or her life span. A special section for tweens and teens is included.

Organizations

The Redwoods Initiative
http://www.redwoodsinitiative.org/
The Redwoods Initiative is a not-for-profit venture focused on family sustainability through wealth education. Their mission is to enable the next generation of families with significant wealth to become fully comfortable with the language of finance and the management of their resources.

Independent Means Inc.
http://www.independentmeans.com
Independent Means is the national leader in providing financial education for children of high-net-worth families. The goal of all the programs is to teach the next generation how to be financially self-reliant while living a life of purpose and passion.

Financial Psychology
Books

Creating Wealth from the Inside Out Workbook
By Kathleen Burns Kingsbury
Written as a client resource, this workbook offers practical information and activities to help clients change how they think and feel

about money. Use with couples to help them learn to identify and talk about their money mindsets.

The Financial Wisdom of Ebenezer Scrooge: 5 Principles to Transform Your Relationship with Money
By Ted Klontz, Rick Kahler, and Brad Klontz
This book teaches readers about money beliefs by using the character Scrooge from the Charles Dickens story. *A Christmas Carol.* Tips and tools are offered to help readers gain insight into their money scripts, how these beliefs impact their financial habits, and how changing their thoughts about money can alter their financial health.

Mind over Money: Overcoming the Money Disorders That Threaten Our Financial Health
By Brad Klontz and Ted Klontz
The authors look at why we overspend, undersave, and have anxiety around money. The reader learns to recognize negative and self-defeating patterns of thinking, and replace them with better, healthier ones that ultimately result in a better relationship with money and wealth.

Money Magic: Unleashing Your True Potential for Prosperity and Fulfillment
By Deborah Price
In this book, the author shows readers how to stop making fear-based money choices and how to transform their relationship with money to obtain the wealth they desire. Using eight money types, the author helps readers understand their relationship with money and offers strategies for changing unhealthy money attitudes and behaviors.

Organizations

Financial Therapy Association
http://www.financialtherapyassociation.com
The Financial Therapy Association is a nonprofit organization dedicated to discussing and researching the cognitive, emotional,

behavioral, relationship, and economic aspects of financial health. They host an annual conference, offer a list of financial therapists and consultants by geographic region, and publish the *Journal of Financial Therapy* on a periodic basis.

Gender Differences
Books

The Female Brain
By Louann Brizendine
Pioneering neuropsychiatrist Dr. Brizendine brings together the latest findings to show how the unique structure of the female brain determines how women think, what they value, how they communicate, and whom they love.

The Male Brain
By Louann Brizendine
In the follow-up book to *The Female Brain*, the author explores the latest findings in neuropsychiatry to show how the unique structure of the male brain influences how men think, what they value, how they communicate, and whom they love.

The End of Men: And the Rise of Women
By Hanna Rosin
In this landmark book, Rosin reveals how this new state of affairs is radically shifting the power dynamics between men and women at every level of society, with profound implications for marriage, sex, children, work, and more.

The Male Factor: The Unwritten Rules, Misperceptions and Secret Beliefs of Men in the Workplace
By Shaunti Feldhahn
Based on a nationwide survey and confidential interviews with more than 3,000 men, the author discusses how men in the workplace tend to think about their female colleagues. Feldhahn also wrote the bestseller *For Women Only: What You Need to Know About the Inner Lives of Men*.

Mental Health and Addictions
Books

To Buy or Not to Buy: Why We Overshop and How to Stop
By April Lane Benson
Drawing on recent research and decades of working with overshoppers, Dr. Benson brings together key insights with practical strategies to provide a self-help program for clients who spend or shop too much.

The Real Dope on Dealing with an Addict: How Addiction Saved My Life
By Meridith Elliot Powell and Beth Brand
This book is written by two sisters who witnessed addiction firsthand. A how-to survival guide for anyone with an addict or alcoholic in his or her life, it contains practical, insider advice for those who love someone with an addiction and want to heal.

Weight Wisdom: Affirmations to Free You from Food and Body Concerns
By Kathleen Burns Kingsbury and Mary Ellen Williams
This book offers simple reflections, vignettes, and everyday analogies that the authors have successfully used with their own clients to counter destructive feelings and shatter distorted ideas of food and weight. Included is a section for parents and loved ones of those afflicted.

Organizations

Alcoholics Anonymous (AA)
http://www.aa.org
AA is a 12-step recovery program aimed at helping its members stay sober and live a fulfilling life. Meetings are free and occur around the globe. The website contains literature and resources on the topic of alcohol addiction.

Depression and Bipolar Support Alliance
http://www.dbsalliance.org
Support meetings, education, and training on depression and bipolar mood disorders are offered on this website. Also offered are resources for families affected by these illnesses.

Gamblers Anonymous

http://www.gamblersanonymous.org/ga/

Gamblers Anonymous offers a 12-step recovery program for individuals who are addicted to gambling, with meetings held in various communities across the globe. The website contains useful data and information for those suffering from this illness.

Multi-Service Eating Disorders Association (MEDA), Inc.

http://www.medainc.org

MEDA is a nonprofit organization dedicated to the prevention and treatment of eating disorders. The website has information on treatment for clients and families as well as educational and support groups.

Narcotics Anonymous (NA)

http://www.na.org

NA is a 12-step recovery program for those affected by drug addiction. Meetings are free and are available globally. The website offers information and resources on the topic.

Nontraditional Couples

Books

Estate Planning for the Blended Family

By L. Paul Hood Jr. and Emily Bouchard

This book outlines estate planning specifically for blended families. It addresses the special concerns and issues that may arise from the process in this special set of circumstances.

Organizations

Pride Planners

http://www.prideplanners.org

Pride Planners, founded in 1999 as a small, informal meeting of planners sharing experiences and concerns, has grown into an organization that provides training for advisors and facilitates referrals for clients looking for qualified financial professionals in their community.

Same Sex Law

http://www.samesexlaw.com

This website is hosted by Frederick Hertz, an attorney in Oakland, California, who provides legal counsel to same-sex partners on the formation and dissolution of their same-sex relationships as well as mediation services. The website contains articles, books, and an informative blog on the legal and financial issues to consider as a gay couple.

Purposeful Planning Institute

http://www.purposefulplanninginstitute.com/

The Purposeful Planning Institute is a membership organization that offers advisors to high-net-worth and ultra-high-net-worth clients, and related professionals (estate attorneys, family wealth consultants, psychologists, CPAs, etc.) education and training on a variety, of issues, including working with nontraditional families and the psychology of money and wealth.

Testing

Moneymax Personality Profile

http://www.kathleengurney.com

Developed by Kathleen Gurney, PhD, the Moneymax Money Personality Profile is a tool used by advisors and coaches to determine clients' money personalities. For a low cost, you can subscribe to the website and receive information and resources as well as access to Gurney's couple's comparison reports.

Financial DNA

http://www.financialdna.com/

Developed by Hugh Massie and his team, Financial DNA tests a client's money personality on several scales. They also offers assessment tools on communication preferences and financial decision making.

Kolbe A Index

http://www.kolbe.com/

This test measures conative thinking. A quick and easy 36-question test provides you and your clients with data on how they get tasks done when they are operating at their optimal level of performance.

Women and Wealth
Books

Ask for It: How Women Can Use the Power of Negotiation to Get What They Really Want
By Linda Babcock and Sara Laschever
This is a good resource for help you understanding why negotiation is challenging for women. It offers a four-phase self-help program, backed by years of research, to help readers identify what they are really worth and teaches them how to develop a strategy to make more money.

Knowing Your Value: Women, Money and Getting What You're Worth
By Mika Brzezinski
This book provides an in-depth look at how women today achieve their deserved recognition and financial worth. Through interviews with prominent women and men, Brzezinski reveals why women are paid less and the pitfalls women face when trying to get paid their worth at work while trying to move up in their field.

How to Give Financial Advice to Women: Attracting and Retaining High-Net-Worth Female Clients
By Kathleen Burns Kingsbury
This practical book helps you understand the wants and needs of affluent female clients and shows you how to appeal to this group of loyal investors. First, it breaks down the psychological fundamentals of women and wealth, and then it outlines the skill set you need to effectively communicate with and advise affluent women.

Moving Forward on Your Own: A Financial Guidebook for Widows
By Kathleen M. Rehl
This practical workbook helps widows be more confident, knowledgeable, and secure about their money matters during this transition.

The Secrets of Six-Figure Women: Surprising Strategies to Up Your Earnings and Change Your Life
By Barbara Stanny
This book explores the traits of financially successful women and offers practical guidance to those women who aspire to increase their wealth.

Women's Worth: Finding Your Financial Confidence
By Eleanor Blayney
This book offers information and practical advice about the fundamentals of financial planning as they apply to women and their specific needs and offers tips for improving financial confidence.

Organizations

Catalytic Women
http://www.catalyticwomen.com
This organization harnesses the economic power of thoughtful, intelligent women who give to our communities. It brings philanthropy professionals together who bring practical experience on helping individuals give wisely and with maximum impact. The programs included are monthly speaking programs, an extensive online library on giving, online forums, list serves, and philanthropic consulting.

Center for Women's Business Research
https://www.facebook.com/CforWBR
The Center for Women's Business Research provides rigorous, data-driven knowledge that advances the economic, social, and political impact of women business owners and their enterprises.

Directions for Women
http://www.DirectionsforWomen.com
This website is dedicated to providing resources for advisors interested in working more effectively with women clients as well as information to empower female clients. Directions hosts circle training and retreats for women financial advisors who want to be

rejuvenated and enhance their ability to better serve and attract women clients.

Learn Vest
http://www.LearnVest.com
The mission of this organization is to help women take control of their finances by increasing their financial literacy, and helping them budget and plan for the future. Learn Vest offers free services as well as low-cost expert advice.

Index

Note: Page references followed by *f* indicate figures.

About the Author

Kathleen Burns Kingsbury is a wealth psychology expert, behavioral change specialist, and author of several books including *How to Give Financial Advice to Women: Attracting and Retaining High-Net-Worth Female Clients* (McGraw-Hill, 2013). She is the founder of KBK Wealth Connection, a company dedicated to training, coaching, and consulting with financial services professionals to improve client communication, retention, and profitability.

As an expert on financial psychology, Kathleen has been quoted by the *Wall Street Journal*, MSNBC's *Today Money*, Forbes's *ForbesWoman*, Thomson Reuters's *Reuters Wealth*, and *Financial Planning Magazine*. Her articles have been published in *Advisors Perspectives*, *American Banker Magazine*, *Financial Advisor*, *Investment and Wealth Monitor*, and *REP Magazine*. In addition, she is a regular contributor for Financial-Planning.com, OnWallstreet.com, and the Women Advisors Forum.

Kathleen serves as a faculty member of the Investment Management Consultants Association's Certified Private Wealth Advisor (CPWA) program and as an adjunct lecturer at the McCallum Graduate School of Business at Bentley University, where she teaches *Psychology in Financial Planning*. She is frequently asked to keynote at industry conferences and has been engaged by financial firms including Pioneer Investments, State Street Global Advisors, TD Ameritrade Institutional, and others as a consultant and trainer.

Kathleen holds a Master's Degree in Psychology from Lesley University and a Bachelor's Degree in Finance from Providence

College. She is a member of the American Association of University Women, the Financial Therapy Association, the National Speakers Association, the Purposeful Planning Institute, and an affiliate member of the Boston Estate Planning Council.

When she is not working, Kathleen is an avid alpine skier who lives for the next powder day. In the off season, she enjoys road and mountain biking, kayaking, and sailing.

For more information about Kathleen and her company, KBK Wealth Connection, please visit the following links:

Website: http://www.kbkwealthconnection.com

Twitter: http://www.twitter.com/kbkspeaks

LinkedIn: http://www.linkedin.com/in/kathleenburnskingsbury

"A great addition to any financial planner's professional bookshelf."

—Rick Kahler, CFP, coauthor of *Conscious Finance* and *The Financial Wisdom of Ebenezer Scrooge*

The essential handbook for connecting with your female clients

Understand the Mindset of Affluent Women

HOW *to* GIVE FINANCIAL ADVICE *to* WOMEN

Attracting & Retaining High-Net-Worth Female Clients

Kathleen Burns Kingsbury
WEALTH PSYCHOLOGY EXPERT

Also available as an e-book.